WORTHWHILE INITIATIVES?

Canadian Mission-Oriented Diplomacy

D1279556

Titles in the *Contemporary Affairs* Series

NUMBER 1
The Big Chill: Canada and the Cold War

NUMBER 2
Knight-Errant? Canada and the Crusade to Ban Anti-Personnel Land Mines

NUMBER 3
Lament for an Army: The Decline of Canadian Military Professionalism

NUMBER 4
The North Atlantic Triangle Revisited: Canadian Grand Strategy at Century's End

NUMBER 5
NORAD: In the New Millennium

NUMBER 6
Worthwhile Initiatives? Canadian Mission-Oriented Diplomacy

NUMBER 7
From Fishermen to Fish: The Evolution of Canadian Fishery Policy

CONTEMPORARY *Affairs* NUMBER 6

WORTHWHILE INITIATIVES?

Canadian Mission-Oriented Diplomacy

Andrew F. Cooper
Geoffrey Hayes

CANADIAN INSTITUTE OF INTERNATIONAL AFFAIRS

INSTITUT CANADIEN DES AFFAIRES INTERNATIONALES

CIIA/ICAI

IRWIN PUBLISHING

Toronto, Canada

Canadian Cataloguing in Publication Data

Worthwhile initiatives?: Canadian mission-oriented diplomacy

(Contemporary affairs series; no.6)
Co-published by the Canadian Institute of International Affairs.
Based on a workshop organized in Feb. 1998 by the Centre on Foreign Policy and
Federalism, University of Waterloo.
Includes bibliographical references and index.
ISBN 0-7725-2825-X

1. Canada — foreign relations — 1945-   . I.Cooper, Andrew Fenton, 1950-   .
II. Hayes, Geoffrey, 1961-   . III. Canadian Institute of International Affairs.
IV. Centre on foreign Policy and Federalism (Waterloo, Ont.) V. Series.

FC635.W67 2000   327.71   C00-930492-4
F1034.2.W67 2000

The Canadian Institute of International Affairs is a national, non-partisan, non-profit organization with a mandate to promote the informed discussion, debate and analysis of foreign policy and international affairs from a Canadian perspective. By virtue of its constitution, the CIIA is precluded from expressing an institutional opinion on these issues. The views expressed in the Contemporary Affairs series are, therefore, those of the author alone.

This work could not have been completed without the generous support of the Social Sciences and Humanities Research Council of Canada.

Cover Photo: Ronny Shinder/Rough Layout
Design by: Sonya V. Thursby/Opus House Incorporated
Typesetting by: Carolyn Sebestyen/Opus House Incorporated
Edited by: Curtis Fahey

Published by
Irwin Publishing Ltd.,
325 Humber College Blvd.,
Toronto, Ontario
M9W 7C3

1 2 3 4   03 02 01 00
Printed and bound in Canada.

This book is dedicated to Irene Majer

Contents

Foreword

"Canadian diplomacy"—is that phrase as much an oxymoron as military intelligence or British cooking? Not so, say the authors of the essays in this excellent collection. Canada is not a superpower and never will be, but weakness can be strength and initiative sometimes can replace power. "Sometimes" is perhaps the key word. For Canada, as for every country, sloppy preparation and poor execution can doom a diplomatic initiative. Public opinion, eager for every sniff of a Canadian triumph, can be totally misguided. And success in one area can often lead to after-shocks in others.

A middle-power, Canada has to be a niche player, to understand what it can and cannot do. The nation needs to avoid preaching moralism, to pretend that Canada is a "moral superpower" while the United States is only a mere superpower. Americans and others (including many Canadians) have become very tired of the preachiness of Canadian foreign policy. It was former U.S. Sectretary of State Dean Acheson who almost forty years ago jeered at Canada as "the Stern Daughter of the Voice of God", and the same complaint could be made today.

The papers here, the product of a Workshop at the University of Waterloo, are hard-headed and clear in their arguments. Canada can do good, but only if it knows what it's doing and how to do it. Good advice for the denizens of the Pearson Buildings.

J.L. Granatstein
Rowell Jackman Resident Fellow
Canadian Institute of International Affairs

Preface

This volume examines the motivations, the techniques, the limitations, and the impact associated with Canadian "mission-oriented" diplomacy. The impulse for Canada to lead—or at least take on a substantial role—in bold international ventures is far from new. Indeed, one of the key features of the statecraft associated with Lester Pearson was a willingness to take on specific initiatives where and when they were required.

What is new is the form, the scope, and the intensity of this "mission-oriented" diplomacy as practised in the 1990s. The initiatives taken on in the period from the late 1940s through to the 1950s were almost exclusively the preserve of the skilled and confident cohort of Department of External Affairs officials. By way of contrast, much of the character of initiatives launched in the 1990s has been shaped by civil society generally and non-governmental organizations (NGOs) more specifically. Getting key non-state actors onside has become as important a determinant for diplomatic progress as the traditional pattern of coalition-building with like-minded countries.

Initiatives have also increased in number. This has led to charges that a degree of selectivity has been lost. Greater familiarity with "mission" diplomacy has bred a sense of diminution if not contempt. The strength of this type of sentiment is witnessed by the mythology surrounding the supposed overuse of this mode of diplomacy in the minds of outside observers. The headline "Worthwhile Canadian Initiative" never actually appeared in an often-cited 1985 *New York Times*' list of the most boring headlines ever printed. But this kind of reference (perpetuated by more than just a Canadian satirical magazine) has contributed to the idea that Canadian initiatives are spawned, not by the objective needs of the national interest, but by the subjective desires of politicians and bureaucrats eager for the same Nobel Peace Prize won by Pearson.

Although prone in the minds of some as being indicative of "initiativeitis," the sheer range of issue-areas encompassing contemporary Canadian "mission" diplomacy is impressive. This diffuse character is highlighted by the case studies chosen for this book. The well-publicized initiative on anti-personnel land mines underscores the continued salience of functional problem-solving in Canadian diplomacy. The initiatives on Zaire/Great Lakes, Nigeria, Cuba, and the Arctic circumpolar region demonstrate the broad scope of geographic focus.

Nor should the intensity level of this activity be minimized. The end of the Cold War may well have brought with it heightened leadership opportunities for countries beyond the traditional big powers. But the erosion of the disciplines associated with bipolarity and the East/West divide has also brought with it some added elements of complexity. One important feature that stands out in all of these case studies is the uncertain and often volatile environment through which Canada has had to stickhandle. The nature and impact of this store of constraints deserves serious treatment, if the impact (or in some cases the non-impact) of these initiatives is to be understood.

The aim of this volume is not to be over-celebratory, nor to bury the Canadian impulse for taking initiatives. What is important to emphasize is a balanced approach, with a careful assessment of where, what, how, and why Canada got it right and/or wrong on a case-by-case basis.

The edited collection grew out of a workshop, organized in February 1998 by the Centre on Foreign Policy and Federalism at the University of Waterloo. This workshop was sponsored by the Canadian Centre for Foreign Policy Development (CCFPD). Special thanks for support of the workshop must go to Steve Lee, as national director of the centre, and to Project Ploughshares, of Conrad Grebel College, University of Waterloo. Thanks also to Emily Stokes-Rees and Joe Campos for their assistance during the conference. Without Whitney Lackenbauer's skills, energy, and enthusiasm, this book would not have come together so quickly and efficiently.

A number of individuals have provided valuable comments and suggestions to improve the nature of the contributions. These include Ken Epps, Bill Graham, MP, Mark Gwozdecky, John Hay, and Ernie Regehr. We would also like to thank Jack Granatstein for his interest in the project. As general editor of the Contemporary Affairs, series, he was instrumental in turning working papers into more concise chapters.

A final note of appreciation goes to John English, an eminent scholar, parliamentarian, and founder of the Centre on Foreign Policy and Federalism. Among John's many talents is his ability to bring out the best in people. Thank you, John, for the many opportunities you have shown us over the years.

Andrew F. Cooper
Geoffrey Hayes

Chapter One

Mission Diplomacy and the "Cult of the Initiative" in Canadian Foreign Policy

Kim Richard Nossal

Since it came to power in November 1993, the Liberal government of Jean Chrétien has put considerable energy into the pursuit of diplomatic initiatives, or what the editors of this volume call Canada's "mission diplomacy." These initiatives have focused on issues as varied as the Helms-Burton legislation passed by the United States Congress; circumpolar cooperation; human rights in Nigeria; Rwandan refugees in Zaire; and the banning of anti-personnel land mines. Other initiatives include efforts to extend the land mines process to cover small weapons; an attempt to secure a ban on the use of child soldiers; and an attempt to create an international criminal court.

Of course, the Chrétien government's initiatives in the mid- and late 1990s are very much in keeping with a long-standing tradition in Canadian statecraft—a tradition that puts a value on seizing the day, taking the initiative, and getting involved to solve a problem that confronts the international community. That, after all, is the essence of "mission diplomacy."

At one level, "mission diplomacy" might seem like somewhat of a tautology. After all, one cannot engage in diplomacy without engaging in the action described by the Latin root, *mittere*, to send off. Indeed, the first definition one comes across for "mission" in the dictionary is "a body of persons sent to conduct negotiations or establish relations with a foreign country." And if we limit ourselves to that meaning of mission, we do indeed have a tautology.

But we should be more interested in the other definitions of "mission." For a mission is not just the body of persons sent off to engage in diplomacy; a mission also refers to the task they have been given to accomplish—it refers to what the people *do* as much as to what they *constitute*. Likewise, we should also remember that a mission can also refer to one's calling, or vocation. And, finally, we should not forget that mission also has a particularly Christian meaning—the spreading of the faith in other lands or territories. In short, once we get beyond the obvious tautological aspects, we get a better sense of why "mission diplomacy" is a useful term to apply to worthwhile Canadian initiatives. For there can be no doubt: in a Canadian context, mission diplomacy has all the elements noted above. It tends to be highly task-oriented; Canadian diplomatic initiatives are designed to solve a very particular (and usually very pressing) problem. Mission diplomacy has also become somewhat of a vocation for Canadians; and indeed there is a certain missionary quality to it.

The various contributions to this volume focus on the particular tasks—in other words, how mission diplomacy actually works in particular situations. This introductory chapter seeks to place the working of Canadian initiatives into a broader context, that is, to examine the setting in which initiatives occur. It thus focuses on two important elements of Canada's mission diplomacy: the vocational and the missionary elements. I also want to focus on how these elements can become a form of addiction, and what impact this addiction can have on foreign policy.

The Vocational Nature of Mission Diplomacy

In 1979 Akira Ishikawa argued that the Canadian approach to foreign policy, marked by what at the time was called the "helpful fixer" tradition, had developed into a kind of Canadian *métier*—something that Canadians did well, enjoyed doing, and were seen as doing well by others in the international system.[1] Indeed, by the time that Ishikawa was writing, a particular style of Canadian diplomacy had become intimately connected with how Canadian foreign-policy makers conceived of their proper role in world politics (and how others in the international system tended to see Canada).

The middle-power activism of the 1950s and 1960s was driven by the belief that Canadian diplomats not only *should* intervene but *could* intervene—and make a difference to world politics. The internationalism of that period was, of course, a reaction by foreign-policy makers to what they perceived was the key failure of Canadian statecraft in the 1930s—the unwillingness to take the initiative, the hesitancy to try to solve international problems. Indeed, the reason that the Suez crisis of 1956 is so important in Canadian foreign policy is that it confirmed for policy makers in Ottawa, both then and later, the essential rightness of this belief. The tremendous success of Canada's secretary of state for external affairs, Lester B. Pearson, in "solving" the dispute created by the Israeli/French/English reaction to the nationalization of the Suez Canal by Gamal Abdel Nasser meant that, after 1956, middle-power diplomacy was intimately bound up in mission diplomacy and diplomatic initiatives. Foreign-policy initiatives quickly became a Canadian vocation.

Indeed, Ishikawa's point was that even those, like Pierre Elliott Trudeau, who came to power trying to resist that pull of the vocation found the attractions overwhelming. Certainly, when one looks at Trudeau's long years in power, one can see "mission diplomacy" from the outset in the late 1960s to that final winter of 1983-4, when he closed out his long prime ministership with the so-called "peace initiative" aimed at reducing tensions between the United States and the Soviet Union. Whether pursuing the issue of arms sales to South Africa at the Commonwealth prime ministers' meeting in Singapore or making the rounds of the great-power capitals at the end of his tenure as prime minister, Trudeau turned out to be deeply attached to the idea of the initiative in foreign policy. To be sure, much of this mission diplomacy was conducted by the prime minister himself or his special foreign policy adviser, Ivan Head.[2] But the impetus that drove Trudeau's initiatives was little different than the impetus that lay behind the initiatives of an earlier era.

If Trudeau's Liberal government ended up pursuing mission diplomacy despite his initial denigration of the "helpful fixing" tradition of Canadian foreign policy, the Progressive Conservative government under Brian Mulroney that took office in the fall of 1984 started off not knowing much about foreign policy at all. But Mulroney and his first secretary of state for external affairs, Joe Clark, turned out to be no less initiative-minded than their predecessors. One can think of initiatives such as the push to sanction South Africa;[3] Clark's involvement in the *Contadora* process in Central America; the push towards the end of the Cold War in the Open Skies initiative; the North Pacific Co-operative Security Dialogue; the efforts to foster confidence in Hong Kong in the years immediately after the Tiananmen massacre; or Mulroney's successful efforts to get President George Bush to use the United Nations in the conflict with Iraq over the Iraqi invasion and annexation of Kuwait.

The Chrétien government came to power in November 1993 actively seeking to avoid the kind of activist foreign policy that had been pursued by the Mulroney government. In fact, Chrétien sought to make a virtue of a minimalist posture in international affairs, distancing himself and his government from the foreign-policy activism of the Mulroney era. In this he was massively helped by André Ouellet, who, before he went to his $300,000-a-year reward heading Canada Post, distinguished himself by attracting rude nicknames in the Department of Foreign Affairs and International Trade, the most memorable being "Mr. Five Per Cent"—for the amount of time that he allegedly spent on foreign policy. But such lassitude or insouciance—it is hard to tell which better captures the Chrétien government's approach to foreign policy during the first year or so—was eventually abandoned. Indeed, the gaggle of Chrétien-era initiatives is eloquent testimony to the degree to which mission diplomacy is alive and well and living in Ottawa.

If we can establish that taking the initiative in international affairs enjoys a long pedigree in Canadian foreign policy, can we conclude that mission diplomacy constitutes a Canadian vocation? I would argue that everything certainly points in this direction: the pride that political leaders and policy makers take in these initiatives; the persistent willingness to engage in worthwhile initiatives year after year; the fact that even those who come to power knowing little about foreign policy (like Mulroney), or who are not inclined toward activism (like Chrétien), or who are actively opposed to foreign-policy initiatives (like Trudeau) all end up pursuing initiatives in their foreign policy.

The Roots of Initiative-Mindedness

What appears to be a relentless and almost deterministic impulse to mission diplomacy in Canadian foreign policy, of course, begs a broader question: Where does Canadian initiative-mindedness come from? I would argue that one can answer that question only when it is asked in different tenses, for what explains worthwhile Canadian initiatives in the past need not necessarily provide useful explanations for what drives similarly worthwhile initiatives today.

In the past, the idea of middle-power activism that is marked by initiatives and mission diplomacy emerged from historical experience. As John W. Holmes pointed out so often in his writing on post-1945 Canadian statecraft, the attachment to a particular kind of middle-power diplomacy came from the personal historical experiences of a generation of Canadian diplomats and politicians, and particularly from the belief that they should not stand by and watch from the sidelines as great-power politics unfolded, transfixed by a mordant fear of domestic politics—as Mackenzie King tended to be.[4]

Suez in 1956 transformed the equation. Canadians keep coming back to Suez, if for no other reason than it was a transformative event. Not only was the initiative of the Canadians really worthwhile in this case, but it was demonstrably successful. Had Canada sat on its hands, other small powers would no doubt have stepped into the breach to try to repair the damage done to relations between the United States and its English and French allies, but Canadian policy makers were uniquely situated to play such a role. The Canadian success at Suez showed that foreign-policy activism and mission diplomacy and taking the initiative actually paid off. In short, Suez legitimized middle-power diplomacy.

But the Suez crisis did much more. It transformed the equation by netting Mike Pearson the 1957 Nobel Peace Prize, the only Canadian to have received such an international honour. It also transformed the domestic political equation. As Don Munton has pointed out, activist diplomacy made for good politics.[5] Certainly there can be no doubt that Canadians enjoyed basking in the warm reflection that only the 23-carat gold of a Nobel medal can provide.

For these reasons, Suez ended up casting a long shadow over Canadian statecraft. We can see its effects most clearly in the various Canadian attempts in the 1960s to pull the same kind of rabbit out of the hat in Vietnam—a desire to take the initiative, to find a way to stop the Americans from embroiling themselves in a conflict that many Canadian foreign-policy makers thought was a major mistake. And, as noted above, we have seen it at work during the Trudeau, Mulroney, and Chrétien eras.

But in these later periods, was the same mixture of motives at work as in 1956? I would argue that, after 1956, the mix was different. From the 1960s to the present, some of the original middle-power calculation is still there—an inchoate sense that it is right and good and just that Canadian governments try to embroil themselves in international matters, instead of doing what would be so easy for us to do—retreat back into North America, taking comfort in the belief that the house is as fireproof as it supposedly was in Senator Raoul Dandurand's time.

As a result, there continues to be a belief that the Canadian government should not simply sit back and watch the unfolding of world affairs from the fastness of North America. Thus, for example, to take a case that is not examined in detail in this book, the government took the view that it would not be right to watch from afar the gruesome slaughters that have marked Algerian politics since the cancellation of the elections in 1992 (as we so easily could have done); rather, it was right and proper to try to do something, anything, to stop the slaughter. So the Chrétien government decided to send an envoy to Algeria to see if Canada could assist the Algerian government in bringing the war between the Groupe islamique armée and the government to an end.

But if there are still elements of the original impetus, there is much more in the mix today. First, expectations now play an important role in shaping mission diplomacy. One of the consequences of Suez was that it created an expectation, particularly among the attentive public in Canada, that a good foreign minister is an initiative-minded foreign minister. Those privileged to be in the chattering classes tend to sneer with various degrees of rudeness at foreign ministers who just sit there, sniffing when a foreign minister does not try to engage in worthwhile Canadian initiatives. Look at how Allan MacEachen, Barbara McDougall, and André Ouellet—foreign ministers who tended to avoid initiatives—will go down in the annals compared with ministers who took the initiative, such as Mitchell Sharp, Joe Clark, and Lloyd Axworthy.

Second, and partly because of this, there is always implicit pressure on a foreign minister, if not the government as a whole, to measure up to the Pearsonian ideal of 1956. That the conditions of the fall of 1956 have never been replicated—and indeed are unlikely to be replicated in the future—appears to make no difference to this pressure.

Third, there is the personal factor, something that we should not dismiss lightly. There is little doubt that the foreign minister of a country who manages to pull off a resolution to a thorny political problem will reap considerable rewards—and not just 7.5 million Swedish crowns. This is not to engage in the kind of cynical analysis so often advanced by the media—that these initiatives can be simply attributed to personal ambition, to the exclusion of other factors. But personal ambition is a factor that should not be totally ignored, either. In Canada, the "Pearson factor" not only "pushes" governments; it also "pulls" ministers into the vortex of hopes that they will be the ones to replicate the Pearsonian feat. And, if nothing else, politicians and political leaders always have their eye on posterity, and how they will be remembered. And there can be little doubt that the ideal remains Lester B. Pearson.

Finally, it is important to put initiative-mindedness in foreign policy into a somewhat broader organizational context. We should recognize that there is in the culture of contemporary organizational leadership a factor that impels those who occupy leadership positions to take the initiative—any initiative. In the era before the Great War, the dominant idea in military science was what was called the cult of the offensive, which placed a premium on attacking the enemy. Today, we can talk about a similar idea that appears to grip all large organizations and seize their leadership—a "cult of the initiative." The leader of an institution that comes to power determined merely to do what the organization has been doing well enough in the past is widely perceived to be a poor leader. On the contrary, a "good" leader, according to the cult of the initiative, is one who avoids inertia, who does something new (invariably described as "exciting" and "innovative"), who takes the initiative, who seizes the day. We can see this dynamic in all organizations. A widespread attachment to the cult of the initiative accounts for the reason why we are treated to an unending diet of faddish ear candy from the leaders of our organizations that focuses on their pursuit of newness, usually coated with numerous millennialist references to the "challenges of the 21st century." Whether it be presidents of universities, or deputy ministers of government departments, or CEOs of multinationals—the need to be (or merely appear to be) on the "cutting edge" requires that one be forever taking the initiative. It is useful to keep in mind that foreign ministers are no less prone to this organizational pathology.

The Pitfalls of Initiative-Mindedness

There is little doubt that, in contemporary Canadian political culture, initiative-mindedness in foreign policy is deemed to be a Good Thing. To question the rightness of taking the initiative draws the criticism that one is too negative, too cynical, too unwilling to get involved, too isolationist. While such risks of naysaying must be acknowledged, it nonetheless can be argued that the cult of the initiative has a number of pitfalls. At least four problems can be identified:

THE LOW ODDS OF SUCCESS

While an initiative-minded foreign minister can draw inspiration from the few successful cases of mission diplomacy as played by small players, in fact the odds of success are not good. Indeed, on the whole, mission diplomacy by governments of smaller states has been quite unsuccessful. One can point to any number of examples where an initiative did not work, was dismissed by the principals, or simply fizzled into embarrassing silence. The initiative taken by the Canadian government in the Great Lakes region of Africa, explored in chapter 6 below, is a good example; Canada's 1997 initiative in Algeria is another. Of course, it can still be asked whether the improbability of success dictates that one should not try. The answer is: it depends on the resources available—and the other costs.

THE HIGH COSTS OF MISSION DIPLOMACY

Mission diplomacy can be costly. These costs include the devotion of human resources to the mission—resources that must, of necessity, be taken from other tasks. And, as the aborted Great Lakes mission demonstrated so clearly, on occasion mission diplomacy requires that a government have at its disposal the costly capital equipment necessary to airlift personnel around the world on short notice. The kind of constabulary force that the Chrétien government has embraced might come with a low price tag, but it has limited Canada's flexibility.

Costs also include the more symbolic costs of relations with other governments. First, there are relations with governments whose behaviour the mission seeks to affect. It is axiomatic that, generally speaking, governments do not like to be interfered with, particularly by smaller states, which are often seen as annoying irritants. Many of the high-profile initiatives undertaken by Canada—Paul Martin's Vietnam War initiatives in the mid-1960s; Trudeau's peace initiative in 1983-4; Mulroney's South Africa initiatives from 1985 to 1987; and Lloyd Axworthy's land-mines initiative of 1996-7—all had negative effects on our relations with close friends, particularly the United States. Indeed, the very title of this book—inspired by an American joke—is a reminder of how other more powerful actors see our "worthwhile initiatives" in the international system.

Second, there are relations with those other smaller governments whose support one needs for the success of the mission—the so-called "like-minded" states (or, as they are sometimes called, not without some irony, the "high-minded"[6]). And here one of the critical costs of mission diplomacy is the tendency of initiative-minded governments to tread on each other's toes. Consider the Cairns Group initiative, and the costs to Australian-Canadian relations that came with that initiative when the two supposedly "like-minded" players discovered that their interests profoundly diverged. Or consider the Asia-Pacific initiatives taken by both Australia and Canada in the late 1980s: the governments in Canberra and Ottawa were constantly stepping on each other's toes. Or consider the cooperative-security initiative of the early 1990s: the only reason why Gareth Evans, Australia's foreign minister from 1988 to 1996, managed to do so well was because Canada in essence pulled out of the field once Joe Clark was shuffled to constitutional affairs and his place was taken by a series of foreign ministers who had little time for the Asia Pacific.[7]

THE PARADOX OF PUBLICITY

This kind of diplomatic initiative contains a deeply contradictory paradox. On the one hand, to be "successful" in political terms, one has to be able to take lots of public credit for the good works created by mission diplomacy. Press releases have to be handed out; briefings, press conferences, and speeches have to be given; photo ops have to be arranged; the mission, in short, has to be "spun." But these requirements create their own problems.

First, diplomacy aimed at resolving contentious and intractable political issues generally works best out of the glare of the limelight, for it is only in secret that the tradeoffs, compromises, and humiliations so necessary for conflict resolution can be arranged. The requirements of diplomacy do not sit well or easily with the requirements of initiative taking.

Second, mission diplomacy demands that the initiative taker take maximum credit. But this is a strategy guaranteed to annoy other actors whose involvement might have been crucial to the successful outcomes. The propensity of Canadians to "spin" the land mines treaty as a particularly *Canadian* initiative provides a good example of how to annoy one's friends. And that, of course, has longer-range consequences for future initiatives: once annoyed, twice shy. Thus, the law of diminishing returns suggests that the longer one is in the mission-diplomacy game, the more likely it is that one will shed supporters.

UNINTENDED CONSEQUENCES

Finally, there is the problem that sticking one's nose into someone else's thorny and intractable problem can produce outcomes that one had not anticipated. Prime Minister Lester B. Pearson discovered this when he took the initiative to prompt President Lyndon B. Johnson to halt the bombing of North Vietnam in 1965. Far from resolving the conflict, Pearson merely stiffened the American resolve—and wrecked his personal relationship with Johnson in the process. The Chrétien government's mission to Algeria in 1997 is another example of this dynamic. Instead of managing to "solve" the Algerian civil war, or even reduce the slaughter, the Canadian mission merely hardened the Algerian government against pressure from the international community.

Conclusion

I argued at the outset that mission diplomacy has become a kind of addiction for those who make Canadian foreign policy. We have seen a tendency on the part of governments in Ottawa to embrace that part of the internationalist credo that activism on the international stage is a Good Thing, and that the kind of passivity pursued by the government of W.L. Mackenzie King in the 1930s is a Bad Thing. To be sure, in the years since the 1950s, that original calculus has changed somewhat. Foreign-policy makers after 1956 perpetually live in the shadow of Lester B. Pearson's performance at Suez, and many are seized with a hope that they will be the ones who might equal that achievement. They are also aware of the expectations entrenched in Canadian political culture that puts a premium on activism in foreign policy. In other words, the original idea that drove international activism may still be there, but it is now overlaid with other considerations.

All too often, it can be argued, this has led to a relentless search for an initiative—any initiative—to embrace. But often the plans served up to ministers hungry for another worthwhile Canadian initiative to deliver to the world are not necessarily carefully considered. As Louis Delvoie notes in the conclusion to this book, the cult of the initiative, like the cult of the offensive, too often demands an impetuous charge, where the adrenaline rush overwhelms a careful thinking through of some of the purposes of an initiative or the conditions for success—or even whether success is possible.

NOTES

FCl.B4

1 Akira Ichikawa, "The 'helpful fixer': Canada's Persistent International Image," *Behind the Headlines* 37 (March 1979), 1–25.

2 J.L. Granatstein and Robert Bothwell, *Pirouette: Pierre Trudeau and Canadian Foreign Policy* (Toronto: University of Toronto Press, 1990); for Trudeau's own "foreign policy memoirs," see Ivan Head and Pierre Elliott Trudeau, *The Canadian Way* (Toronto: McClelland & Stewart, 1995).

3 This is best explored in Linda Freeman, *The Ambiguous Champion: Canada and South Africa in the Trudeau and Mulroney Years* (Toronto: University of Toronto Press, 1997).

4 This is most fully outlined in John W. Holmes, *The Shaping of Peace: Canada and the Search for World Order, 1943-1957*, 2 vols. (Toronto: University of Toronto Press, 1979, 1982).

5 Don Munton, "Middle power and Canadian foreign policy," paper presented to the Canadian Political Science Association, Montreal, 1980.

6 Fen Osler Hampson and Maureen Appel Molot, "The new 'can-do' foreign policy," in Hampson and Molot, eds., *Canada Among Nations 1998: Leadership and Dialogue* (Toronto: Oxford University Press, 1998), 2.

7 See Kim Richard Nossal, "Middle Power Diplomacy in the Changing Asia-Pacific Order: Australia and Canada Compared," in Richard Leaver and James L. Richardson, eds., *Charting the Post-Cold War Order* (Boulder, Colo.: Westview Press, 1993), 210-33.

Chapter Two

Niche Diplomacy and Mission-Oriented Diplomatic Behaviour: A Critical Assessment

Heather A. Smith

Introduction

In the last several years the Canadian government has been involved in a series of well-publicized and high-profile international activities. Most recently, newspaper headlines and Department of Foreign Affairs statements have focused on the achievement of the land mines treaty. Other high-profile Canadian initiatives have involved circumpolar cooperation, intervention in a war-ravaged Rwanda, and sanctions against the Nigerian government. These initiatives, all of which are addressed in this collection, may mark a new era in Canadian foreign policy—or do they?

This chapter will raise some questions about the theory and practice that informs these "worthwhile initiatives." The first section of the chapter provides an analytical framework for niche diplomacy, which arguably guides Canada's recent foreign-policy behaviour. The language of niche diplomacy and the similarly conceived idea of mission-oriented behaviour did not develop in a vacuum. An analytical framework provides a context to understand how these concepts affect the wider practice of Canadian foreign policy. The second section of the chapter describes niche diplomacy in practice. The penultimate section assesses the practical and theoretical strengths and weaknesses of this type of diplomacy. While both strengths and weaknesses are identified, it will be seen that the weaknesses outweigh the strengths. Niche diplomacy, if it is to guide Canadian foreign policy, must be given considerably more thought.

Canadian Foreign Policy: The Context

The following framework offers the necessary context to understand how the initiatives under examination were developed. It has three essential components, beginning with Kim Nossal's concept of the dominant idea.[1] The dominant idea highlighted here is managed internationalism. Flowing from the dominant idea is the second element, the strategy. In this instance the focus is on niche diplomacy, although there is some reference to mission diplomacy. Finally, arising out of the combination of the dominant ideas and the strategy is the foreign-policy behaviour.

The dominant idea of managed internationalism denotes a merging of traditional notions of middle power with a two-dimensional vision of management. There remains a broad commitment to the ideal of internationalism, which includes an emphasis on dialogue, compromise, and mediation as well as the promotion of democracy, peace, prosperity, and good governance. But this is internationalism in its ideal. In practice it is constrained by and redefined by the management component of managed internationalism.

The first dimension of management is associated with a worldview grounded in liberal economics and infused with realist assumptions about national interest. It is evident in the ever-present focus on the government's fiscal constraints. The second dimension of management gives expression to a desire for certainty and regularity in a world in flux and is epitomized by the quest for a rule-based international order. While the promotion of a rule-based order does provide for some security for states such as Canada, this desire for certainty and regularity must be seen as attempt to reaffirm and re-establish Canada's place in the world. This element of management suggests a degree of insecurity about Canada's place in the world.

Managed internationalism is easily observed in the notion of human security. Recognizing the complexity of the human environment and the interplay of forces that affect our security, human-security challenges narrow military definitions by including the promotion of prosperity, the protection of fundamental human rights, and the provision of environmental well-being as central tenets of security. In keeping with managed internationalism, efforts to pro-

mote human security are associated with Pearsonian internationalism. The management dimensions are also apparent. Human security is seen as fiscally responsible. "There is a consensus that such a
broader orientation can best be achieved—at least cost, and to best
effect—through approaches that broaden the response to security
issue beyond military options."[2] Consistent with the second dimension of managed internationalism, human security is also associated
with Canadian identity and our sense of where we fit in the world.
"This internationalist vocation is still what gives us our identity and
an enviable place in the world community."[3]

Arising from managed internationalism are strategies such as
niche diplomacy and mission diplomacy. Niche diplomacy is associated with the work of Andrew Cooper and Evan Potter,[4] who argue,
in separate articles, that in an era of fiscal constraint Canadian foreign policy needs to move away from diffuse internationalism. Canada must be more selective and focus on particular issue areas where
there is Canadian expertise and/or a comparative advantage. Suggested niches include peace building, human rights, particularly
women's rights and children's rights, and the protection of natural
resources, to name a few. Our policy initiatives should be, in the
words of liberal economics, effective and efficient. The aim is to
achieve maximum impact.

A part of this strategy includes the devolution of policy making to
non-governmental organizations with the aim of drawing on some of
their expertise. The value of a more discrete foreign policy is that it
counters the perceived commitment-credibility gap that arises from
Canadian foreign-policy makers trying to do everything. Essentially,
we are told to focus our energies in areas that promote and support
Canada's national interest. Niche diplomacy calls for a narrowing of
Canadian foreign policy based on a set of broad criteria—maximum
impact, national interest, effectiveness—that appear to be driven by
a liberal-economic logic coupled with a traditional-realist sense of
preservation and protection of the state's interests.

Mission diplomacy as defined by Richard Higgott is "diplomacy
when and where you need it."[5] A response to the cost of more diffuse
diplomacy, this results-oriented diplomacy has three components.
First, mission-oriented diplomacy is characterized by functional lead-

ership and coalition building. Similar to niche diplomacy, mission diplomacy sees the state in entrepreneurial terms, portraying its function as that of a catalyst or facilitator which draws on national-policy communities. The second component is the inclusion of, and the provision of an enhanced role for, NGOs. Third, this diplomacy is characterized by issue linkage.

Is mission-oriented diplomacy the same thing as niche diplomacy? The two concepts bear many similarities. Functional leadership, the inclusion of NGOs in the policy process, and an emphasis on entre-preneurial and technical skills are common to both definitions. Is this a case of a proliferation of terms denoting the same thing? A close look at Cooper's work suggests that niche diplomacy and mis-sion-oriented diplomacy might not be the same. Cooper implies that niche selection, if not niche diplomacy, takes place in middle powers that might otherwise exhibit different behaviour. Mission diplomacy, or what Cooper calls mission-oriented diplomatic behaviour, is close-ly associated with Australia and Sweden and heroic efforts. Does niche diplomacy imply behaviour other than heroic? This lack of clarity must be resolved. It is assumed here that mission-oriented be-haviour is preceded by niche selection, or a niche diplomatic strate-gy, and associated with heroic efforts. Mission-oriented behaviour is one possible outcome of a niche diplomatic strategy. But if mission-oriented behaviour is informed by the same logic articulated by Cooper and Potter in their discussion of niche diplomacy, it is then open to the same criticisms as niche diplomacy, which will be dis-cussed shortly.

We turn now to the third and final element of the framework. For the definition of the behavioural component we draw on the work of Cooper, building on previous joint work with Richard Higgott and Nossal.[6] Two behavioural roles of particular importance to our dis-cussion of initiatives are the catalyst and the facilitator. Catalyst be-haviour is epitomized by attempts to generate interest around spe-cific issue areas. The facilitator focuses on activities such as "planning, convening and hosting of meetings, setting priorities for future activity and drawing up rhetorical declarations and mani-festos."[7] To this we can add the scope and intensity of diplomacy. Scope ranges from diffuse to discrete and intensity ranges from routine to heroic. Routine diplomacy is associated with a "low-key, consensus-oriented style ... [with] a heavy emphasis on institution building together with managerial skills, whether of a formal or informal nature," whereas a heroic style is associated with "public diplomacy and risk taking."[8]

The importance of including this component to the setting is that in many of the cases under scrutiny Canada has played the role of the catalyst and/or facilitator. This provides for a degree of continuity across the cases. More important, however, is the identification of Canada with the diffuse and routine. Niche diplomacy is premised on selectiveness and some of the initiatives under investigation may have the qualities of heroic intensity. Does this mean that discrete scope inclines states towards heroic action? And, if Canada is typically associated with the diffuse and the routine, is there now a shift in Canadian foreign policy? This question cannot be resolved within the parameters of this chapter, but it is worth further consideration. At this point we turn our attention to niche diplomacy in practice.

Niche Diplomacy in Practice

Adopted by the minister of foreign affairs, Lloyd Axworthy, the term niche has been applied to specific areas such as the strategy of "working from within" in the context of human rights, peace building, and international communications. Niche diplomacy or niche selection has been built into these broader themes. For example, built into human security is a set of non-traditional threats such as poverty, human-rights abuses, terrorism, and environmental degradation. Focusing on human rights, one can identify priority issues such as children's rights, particularly child labour. Niches are then identified within the issues given priority status. Canada's niche or area of specialization in the context of human rights is defined as working from within. A similar pattern can be identified when we refer to peace building. Peace building, like human rights, is embedded in human security. In recognition of the enormity of the concept of peace building, niches are then selected.

Niches are few and far between in government statements and so one may think that, in keeping with the prescriptions of Cooper and

Potter, Canada is becoming more selective. The problem is that the logic of the niche selection seems at times counterintuitive, as is the case with children's rights. Moreover, it appears that the potential exists for Canadian foreign policy to practise heroic behaviour without substance or, alternatively, to continue with a diffuse scope while at the same time identifying niches. This potential, and the issue of niche selection, will be discussed further in the next section.

Strengths and Weaknesses of Niche Diplomacy and Mission-Oriented Behaviour

Given that some form of niche diplomacy has become part of the Canadian foreign-policy discourse, it is incumbent upon us to think carefully about the implications of this idea and how it is given expression in the various initiatives under examination in this collection. This section highlights some of the strengths and weaknesses associated with niche diplomacy and foreshadows some of the points that will be raised in forthcoming chapters. The analysis is by no means exhaustive. We begin with the strengths.

First, practically and theoretically, a focus on middle-power initiatives reaffirms Higgott's argument that "there are issues at stake in the global and economic orders other than those of the three or four dominant actors."[9] Issues such as child labour, land mines, and ethnic strife, designated as priorities by the Canadian government, are important. While we may have some reservations about the substance behind these priorities, one would be hard pressed to say that they are unimportant. Perhaps it is possible to put aside our cynicism about the motivations behind the initiatives and ask whether or not we are better off because of the international cooperation that has taken place. They may not be the high politics of the past, but they are issues that affect people around the world, on a daily basis.

Second, as the cases discussed in this book reveal, middle powers matter. Canada has played and continues to play crucial roles in facilitating early cooperation on many issues. Because of Canadian political will and diplomatic skill, a land mines treaty was successfully negotiated. The personal diplomacy of the prime minister forced world attention on the tensions in Rwanda.

Third, we are reminded, theoretically and practically, that middle power is not a fixed universal.[10] Labelling makes things neat but it is not always effective. By showing that middle-power behaviour is varied and that functional leadership is possible, we show that Canada is more than a mediator and a peacekeeper. We may still be these things, but the changing international system offers Canada an opportunity to play different roles in the international system.

Fourth, and finally, niche diplomacy has the potential to foster internal and external democratization of foreign policy. NGOs and other civil-society actors are integral to many of the recent foreign-policy initiatives. If NGOs and citizens are actively and legitimately included in the policy process, then there is a possibility of addressing the growing disconnection between public and government. It could help to rebuild civil society and thus counter the potentially disintegrating forces of globalization. Moreover, it is this characteristic of recent initiatives that may make them unique and herald a new era in Canadian foreign policy. The tentativeness of this claim rests on the fact that there are also many limitations to niche diplomacy. It may not fulfil its promise.

Seven weaknesses may be noted. The first weakness builds on the discussion in the previous section. The language of niche diplomacy and mission-oriented diplomacy is sometimes confusing and vague. As noted earlier, niche diplomacy and mission-oriented diplomacy seem to describe the same thing, but are they the same thing? In a similar vein we can ask, what constitutes national interest? How do we measure effectiveness? How do we understand success? Many of these issues are raised in this collection.

Second, we need to ask whether niche diplomacy is new. Is it somehow different from initiatives in the past? The Mulroney administration initiated efforts in the area of child labour and circumpolar cooperation, and so it cannot be said that initiatives are unique to the present government. Is this simply a case of "old wine in new bottles"?

Third, to what extent are Canadian initiatives nothing more than "the flavour of the day," designed to respond to and benefit from media attention? Child labour is a possible example. Canada was involved in this issue area prior to the election of the Liberal government in 1993; however, it seemed to rise on the international agenda after a series of high-profile press events involving Kathy Lee Gifford. It appears to have been pushed onto the Canadian agenda in part by the action of one boy, Craig Keilberger, in 1996. If Canadian diplomatic initiatives are simply public-relations opportunities, then there is a possibility that these initiatives will lack substance and, in the long term, prove unsustainable. The rashness also seems to counter the implied logic of niche diplomacy where one should select carefully, not hastily.

A fourth potential problem arises from the results-orientation of these strategies. Who are the results for? Are the initiatives designed for public consumption with an end to enhancing domestic credibility? Are the initiatives designed to bolster Canada's international reputation with the aim of showing the world that we are still a player, a good international citizen, or a leader? Who are the clientele?[11] If the initiatives are motivated simply by Canadian self-interest, we are unlikely to meet the needs of those we are trying to aid.

Fifth, we must point to potential problems related to niche selection and deselection. There must be care in the selection of niches. Ad hoc, heroic crusades driven by a quest for the Nobel Prize may have limited long-term value. If Canada continues to select niches such as human rights, particularly "working from within," and if Canada falters in its leadership on some of the recent initiatives, then the commitment-credibility gap will widen. This will further serve to undermine any sense of security that we may be trying to achieve.

In terms of niche deselection, what happens when an issue area no longer meets the criteria of a niche? Climate change, for example, was an issue marked for Canadian leadership by Brian Mulroney and yet the Chrétien government scrambled at the recent conference in Kyoto, Japan, to cobble together an internationally credible position. Climate change became costly when it appeared to affect economic competitiveness. What happens when other initiatives no longer serve our national interest? What happens when we can no longer sustain our commitment to a particular issue area? It is possible to counter that our resources and skills are limited, but does that mean that middle powers can then randomly remove themselves from niches once the market has filled up with other producers? The analogy between the market and diplomacy can only be taken so far. Initiatives come with obligations. At stake is international credibility.

Sixth, niche diplomacy has the potential to be elitist and exclusive. If members of civil society are to be included in the foreign-policy process, that process must be genuinely open to their views. The urge to manage politically the activities and opinions of societal actors must be resisted by foreign-policy makers because otherwise the efforts at democratization will be viewed sceptically.

Seventh, and finally, niche diplomacy obscures the personal and legitimizes balance-sheet diplomacy. We are told that foreign policy should aim to achieve maximum impact. Cooper and Potter speak to us in economic terms: comparative advantage, efficient, effective, fiscal restraint, entrepreneurial, selective. The language and discourse of liberal economics must be tempered because otherwise any hope inspired by the precepts of humane internationalism will be undermined as the human is taken out of the equation.

Conclusion

Niche diplomacy and mission-oriented diplomatic behaviour may be seen as an alternative to the diffuse (and, by extension, fiscally irresponsible) internationalism of the past. The selection of niches does have the potential to provide for a more focused, rigorous Canadian foreign policy. We can play a leadership role in some international issue areas. Choices clearly have to be made. Yet there remains a tension between the desire to maintain the legacy of internationalism while at the same time reducing expenditures, protecting our national interest, and achieving maximum impact. Results-oriented diplomacy seems to cater to the Canadian elites—not the people who really need our support. Niche diplomacy, moreover, has the potential to obscure the personal from our diplomacy—people become numbers on a balance sheet. This is to be avoided.

In spite of these concerns, niche diplomacy is likely to appeal to the policy makers in Ottawa. It is a strategy that is informed by the dominant idea of the day, managed internationalism, and it supports the prevailing norms of the international system. Even if it is applied in a rather ad hoc manner, it is unlikely to disappear from the 1990s' dictionary of Canadian foreign policy.

NOTES

1   Kim Richard Nossal, *The Politics of Canadian Foreign Policy*, 2nd ed. (Scarborough, Ont.: Prentice-Hall Canada, 1989), chapter 5.

2   Government of Canada, *Canada in the World* (Ottawa: Canadian Council for International Cooperation, 1995), 25.

3   Lloyd Axworthy, "Between Globalization and Multipolarity: The Case of a Global Humane Canadian Foreign Policy," <http://www.dfait-maeci.gc/english/foreignp/humane.html>, 11.

4   See Andrew F. Cooper, "In Search of Niches: Saying 'Yes' and Saying 'No' in Canada's International Relations," in *Canadian Foreign Policy* 3/3 (winter 1995), 1-13, and Evan H. Potter, "Niche Diplomacy as Canadian Foreign Policy," *International Journal*, LII (winter 1996–7), 25–38.

5   Richard Higgott, "Issues, Institutions and Middle Power Diplomacy: Action and Agendas in the Post-Cold War Era," in Andrew F. Cooper, ed., *Niche Diplomacy: Middle Powers after the Cold War* (New York: St. Martin's Press, 1997), 37.

6   See Andrew F. Cooper, "Niche Diplomacy: A Conceptual Overview," in *Niche Diplomacy*; Andrew F. Cooper, Richard A. Higgott, and Kim Richard Nossal, *Relocating Middle Powers: Australia and Canada in a Changing World Order* (Vancouver: University of British Columbia Press, 1993).

7   Cooper, "Niche Diplomacy: A Conceptual Overview," 9.

8   Ibid., 10-11.

9   Higgott, "Issues, Institutions and Middle Power Diplomacy," 35.

10   See Robert Cox, "Middle Powermanship, Japan and Future World Order," in Robert W. Cox and Timothy J. Sinclair, eds., *Approaches to World Order* (New York: Cambridge University Press, 1996), 242.

11   This point is made by Martin Rudner in "Canada in the World: Development Assistance in Canada's New Foreign Policy Framework," *Canadian Journal of Development Studies*, 17/2 (1996), 216.

Chapter Three

The Land mine Initiative:
A Canadian Initiative?

John R. English

"All serious foreign policy," Henry Kissinger once declared, "must begin with the need for survival."[1] This classic realist statement has not been posted above the desks of Canadian prime ministers and foreign ministers for most of the twentieth century. Canadian foreign policy, one might argue, was postmodern at its creation. In January 1919 Sir Robert Borden went to the Paris Peace Conference to represent a bitterly divided nation that had lost over 60,000 soldiers in the bloodiest war it ever fought. South Africa and Australia wanted German colonies, Ireland greater independence, and New Zealand more trade. After brief warm dreams of grabbing some West Indian islands, Borden began his work with neither the "need for survival" nor dreams of expansion foremost in his mind. He wrote in his diary: "It was largely a question of sentiment. Canada got nothing out of the War but recognition."[2]

And recognition is all that Borden got out of his long months in Paris; "recognition" was the sole reward for Canada's astonishing sacrifice of soldiers and national unity in the First World War. Canada signed the peace treaty, won a seat at the League of Nations and the International Labour Organization, and convinced the British that they should occasionally pay attention to what the dominions did. These accomplishments contributed nothing to "national survival." Indeed, Canada quickly came to believe that a League with the teeth of sanctions might itself threaten "national survival" and argued for a League that was ceremonial rather than substantial. The best-known Canadian "initiative" of the inter-war period, W.A. Riddell's attempt to impose sanctions on Mussolini's Italy in 1935, ended embarrassingly with Mackenzie King's complete repudiation of the hapless Riddell and the collapse of the sanction initiative. Riddell and Arnold Toynbee later claimed that "Mussolini's defeat of the 'oil sanction' made inevitable the Second World War." Perhaps it did; more likely it was one of many contributing factors.

What is certain is that in 1939 Britain and Canada, unprepared psychologically, militarily, and politically, entered a war that, within a year, did threaten "national survival."[3] Loring Christie and O.D. Skelton, King's senior advisers on foreign policy who were "realists" before Hans Morgenthau, despaired when King and his cabinet (with one dissenter) made the decision to go to war in September 1939. They knew, in Borden's 1919 words, that entry into the Second World War was not a matter of survival; it would be "largely a matter of sentiment." Even though entry into war in 1939 must be seen, realistically, as a repudiation of Borden's efforts in 1919 and of King's policies between the wars, neither receives failing grades for their work as Neville Chamberlain and, until recently, Woodrow Wilson usually have. According to a *Maclean's* poll of scholars and others, King was Canada's best prime minister, and Borden, despite his domestic disasters, is one of the top because he won "recognition" for Canada.[4] The result is unsurprising. In 1998 an Angus Reid poll indicated that Jean Chrétien's "highest rating by far is for his representation of Canada in international affairs," which in 1993 the Opposition had identified as his "Achilles' heel." In reporting on the poll, Edward Greenspon wrote: "The extraordinarily strong approval of his work abroad perhaps helps explain why Mr. Chrétien spends so much time on the road. Even in Quebec, his positives outweigh his negatives by 41 percentage points for his work on the international stage." [5]

From Borden's search for recognition in Paris through Lester Pearson's Nobel Prize-winning efforts in 1956 and Pierre Trudeau's wanderings for peace in 1983-4 to Lloyd Axworthy's land mine campaign of 1997, one finds a common thread in the understanding of the importance of sentiment and the political value of international recognition. In treating these initiatives, one might well take the postmodernist stance that identity was regarded as an effect of foreign policy rather than that Canadian foreign policy reflected a stable, existing condition of being. While Kim Nossal is correct to emphasize that Pearson and his colleagues in foreign affairs reacted against Mackenzie King's inaction in the 1930s, a close reading of the correspondence and memoranda of Pearson, Escott Reid, Charles Ritchie, and others of the "Golden Age" reveals that they, like King, understood foreign policy not so much as the reflection of national identity as its creator. This understanding is, as Nossal argues, a response to domestic politics, but it is much broader. After all, the diplomats' complaint against King was his slavish devotion to the false god of public opinion. Domestic politics reflects what is. Pearson's post-war foreign policy, however, was intuitive not deductive, an expression not of what Canada was but what it might yet be. Nowhere is this quality clearer than in Pearson's friendly debate with the "realist" diplomat, Maurice Pope, who kept asking why on earth Canada was active where its "interests" were so few. And when Pearson encountered the hard edge of American "realism" in the approaches of another friend, Secretary of State Dean Acheson, his responses baffled and eventually angered the American.

Were it not for geography, Acheson wrote in the mid-1960s, "America might not grasp Canada at all for sheer difficulty in figuring out what Canada is." In his essay, "Canada: 'Stern Daughter of the Voice of God,'" Acheson claimed that "Americans—and, perhaps, Canadians, too—do not have much of an idea of what this generic noun Canadian describes, if it describes anything." He pointed to a survey of Canadians' views on world affairs that found Canadians favouring a hard line against the Communist bloc while opposing more foreign aid and peaceful coexistence. These views, according to the survey, were diametrically opposed to those of politicians. Why? Acheson answers shrewdly:

> For [Canadian politicians] there is a strong incentive to seek success and reputation in external rather than internal affairs. The extreme delicacy of the relations between Canada's "two founding peoples" has quite understandably made the present policy of "co-operative federalism" concentrate on keeping the country united and cautious in domestic innovation ...

In "the vast external realm," however, the Canadian politician can and does appear with more panache. A leading Canadian politician has remarked that a representative of a middle-sized power has advantages: He is listened to, but not held responsible for results; thus, he can acquire reputation and honors, while blame for failure goes to those possessed of means and power.

Acheson's remarks bear the resentment of an American "realist" who has endured one too many Canadian initiatives, yet they also reveal a good understanding of the motivations of Canadian policy makers and diplomats.[6]

The editor of the book in which Acheson's essay appeared was Livingston Merchant, former ambassador of the United States to Canada. When ambassador, Merchant quarrelled with External Affairs minister Howard Green about Green's anti-nuclear policies. Nevertheless, when the election came in 1962, Merchant sent a dispatch to Washington in which he argued, rather surprisingly, that "Canada after [the 1962 election] would be a stauncher, more consistent, and reliable ally and understanding friend with Mr. Diefenbaker back in power." To be sure, Green was a bother, but he "represents a powerful political asset as an honest, homespun, stand-up-to-giants idealist."[7] No one understood Canadian "ambivalence" better than Henry Kissinger who brilliantly set out the case for Canadian "exceptionalism." For Canadians, "serious foreign policy" did not begin with the struggle for survival: "Convinced of the necessity of co-operation, impelled by domestic imperatives toward confrontation, Canadian leaders had a narrow margin for manoeuvre that they [have] utilized with extraordinary skill."[8]

The "Achilles' heel" that has become a golden thumb for Jean Chrétien puzzles many Canadians. On the same week when the Reid poll indicated that Chrétien's greatest asset was his performance on the international stage, the Ottawa *Citizen*, in an article entitled "Canada's fall from grace on the world stage," reported that critics within the Department of Foreign Affairs and International Trade (DFAIT) and within the academic community use words such as "irrelevant, out-of-step and dilettantish" in speaking about Canadian foreign policy.[9] The major Canadian academic study of the land mine campaign bears the title *Knight Errant?* and castigates the Canadian government for its refusal to consider the importance of land mines for its military and for the offence that its "idealism" in the anti-land mine "crusade" gave to Americans and others. A military historian denounced the land mine campaign as "simplistic and emotional," while the editor of *Peacekeeping and International Relations*, a publication emanating from the Pearson Peacekeeping Centre (which is supported by Foreign Affairs), attacked the Canadian land mine campaign as simply "puffery" and without worth.[10]

What was its worth? Was Canada in reality a "knight-errant" or simply a "good soldier" that joined a successful campaign? Has Canada, through its reckless enthusiasm, tilted that essential balance which Kissinger described so well between the domestic need for confrontation with the United States, on the one hand, and the realistic necessity of cooperation, on the other, towards confrontation?

The campaign against anti-personnel land mines (APL) was not a Canadian initiative. The campaign began at the beginning of the 1990s when International Committee of the Red Cross (ICRC) surgeons persuaded the ICRC president that the proliferation of APLs had created an epidemic, a "scourge" as real as any dreaded disease. Convinced by his staff, ICRC President Cornelio Sommaruga went beyond the traditional mandate of his organization to call for a "total ban on the production, export and use of anti-personnel mines," which, he argued, was "the only effective solution to the humanitarian catastrophe they have caused." His efforts and those of his organization to amend the 1980 United Nations Convention on Certain Conventional Weapons (CCW) were indefatigable. There were numerous conferences in which the ICRC used its quasi-official status and traditional links with the military forces of sovereign states to urge military officers to confront the question of whether the military utility of land mines was justified given the tens of thousands of innocent civilians who were their victims. When a 1994 conference in Geneva of "experts" reached no conclusion, the ICRC persisted. In 1996 the organization published another study, *Anti-personnel Land mines: Friend or Foe*, in which ten military officers agreed that the "limited military utility of AP mines is far outweighed by the appalling humanitarian consequences of their use in actual conflicts."[11]

While working with military experts and others, the ICRC spent millions of dollars producing videos, pamphlets, and publications attacking the "hidden killers." As the ICRC campaigned with increasing vigour in 1994 and the spring and summer of 1995, the Department of National Defence was rejecting the request of Foreign Minister André Ouellet for support of a United States resolution in the United Nations which would commit signatories to an eventual elimination of APLs.[12]

This United States resolution owed much to the efforts of Vermont Democratic Senator Patrick Leahy, who had managed to convince the United States Senate in 1992 that the United States should ban the export of land mines for one year, a bill that Republican President George Bush signed. Leahy worked closely with a prominent American non-governmental organization (NGO), the Vietnam Veterans of America Foundation (VVAF), whose president, fellow Democrat Bobby Muller, linked his organization with a German group, Medico International, to establish the International Campaign to Ban Land mines (ICBL). In 1992 a fund for victims established within US AID, which was often referred to as the "Leahy fund," contributed directly to the work of the ICBL. Hopes billowed later that year when Bill Clinton won the election and the European Union announced a moratorium on the export of land mines. In 1993 Handicap International, a French ICBL partner, convinced the French government to request that the UN convene a conference to consider a ban on land mines. Writing in *Foreign Affairs* in 1994, UN Secretary General Boutros Boutros-Ghali termed the "land mine crisis" a "humanitarian disaster" and called upon nations to follow the United States and the European Union in enforcing a ban on exports.[13]

The Clinton administration asked its ambassador to the United Nations, Madeline Albright, to introduce a resolution calling on states to follow the US and EU lead. The resolution was adopted unanimously by the General Assembly in December 1993. The following year, Clinton went before the General Assembly and called upon all nations to work together for an ultimate elimination of land mines. Although critics rightly commented that the United States was not yet willing to commit itself to a APL ban, few then would have dissented from the US official Thomas McNamara's claim that "the Clinton administration's initiatives and persistence have placed this problem high on the international agenda."[14] Those who studied the problem turned to the State Department official publication *Hidden Killers: The Global Problem with Uncleared Land mines*, which claimed that land mines "may be the most toxic and widespread pollution facing mankind."[15] Although the United States did abstain on the UN resolution setting up the review conference, it argued strongly in favour of observer status for groups such as the ICBL which were calling for a total ban. Former Secretary of State Cyrus Vance and Ambassador Herbert Okun, who favoured such a ban, argued that the US proposals for the review conference did not go far enough but added that they did stand "in sharp contrast to the modest proposals offered by other governments."[16]

Neither the Canadian government nor Canadian NGOs were going far at this time. Canada could not join France in 1993 in the call for a review conference on the CCW review conference because it had not yet ratified that convention. No Canadian experts attended the ICRC "experts" meetings in 1993 and 1994, and one finds no Canadian presence in *Clearing the Fields*, a report on the major international conference in 1994 which studied the land mine question. As noted above, the Department of Foreign Affairs was trying to have Canadian policy catch up to that of the United States in terms of an export moratorium. There was little domestic pressure for Canada to take up the anti-APL cause, and Mines Action Canada lacked the funding of the US campaign where the Vietnam Veterans of America Foundation gave $4.5 million to support the campaign. Most of those funds, it should be noted, came from US AID.[17]

The review conference came and delivered little. The Clinton administration stumbled in the spring of 1996. Although prominent officials such as Madeline Albright strongly argued for continued US leadership, election-year politics produced hesitation. Clinton's May 1996 statement, which supported a ban with certain limits, disappointed ban proponents. Others came forward to set the standard, such as Belgium, which announced its adherence to a total ban. Canada's position had shifted in 1995, in part because the United Nations had published a list of countries which adhered to an export moratorium and, wrongly, had included Canada. The Department of National Defence agreed that the embarrassment of pointing out the UN error was unthinkable and, reluctantly, consented to an export ban. With this error, the "Canadian initiative" began.

Canada "came lately" but dramatically. The critical decision occurred in October 1996 when Foreign Affairs Minister Lloyd Axworthy decided to issue an invitation to states to return to Ottawa a year later to sign a treaty banning APLs. The ironies were rich. The United States, which had argued for a NGO presence at the CCW review conference and which had indirectly funded American NGO activity, opposed the NGO presence at Ottawa. The French, who had called for the review conference in 1993, were the subject of a withering attack by Americans Jody Williams and Senator Leahy, which stiffened the resolve of the Canadians to go ahead with the invitation that Axworthy issued at the conference's conclusion. When told of the risks and the opportunity, Axworthy reportedly told his officials: "It's the right thing. Let's do it."[18]

Why did it succeed? In answering these questions, the criteria offered in Louis Delvoie's article offer valuable guidance. The initiative did not enjoy the "wholehearted support" of the Canadian government. The Department of National Defence and, reportedly, some Foreign Affairs officials had doubts. Nevertheless, Axworthy could act with confidence because the prime minister was on his side. In 1994 Chrétien, at the request of ICRC president Sommaruga, had raised the question of a land mine ban at the G7 meeting in Naples. Without Chrétien's sympathy, the initiative would have passed to other countries or would have failed. Chrétien's good relationship with Clinton—he "kidded" the American president about his failure to sign the Ottawa Treaty—permitted Canada more freedom than was the case with Trudeau's peace initiative in the 1980s. Moreover, Chrétien and, of course, Axworthy knew that Albright, Leahy, many senior American officials, and probably Hilary Clinton were supportive of an APL ban. Far from getting a sign to "quit," Canada received encouragement from important voices in Congress, the media, and, privately, the administration. Its critics, Jesse Helms and the *Wall Street Journal*, were the usual ones.

The purposes of the initiative were, as Delvoie recommends, "clear and simple." The argument for a complete ban, which was accompanied by powerful visual evidence of young bodies torn to shreds by land mines, was enormously effective. Its strength put its opponents on the defensive. It may have been "simplistic and emotional," as critic Dean Oliver claims, but it was understandable by Canadians and their parliamentary representatives. In a fragmented Parliament, members were unanimous in supporting the government's policy on the APL ban, and this unanimity was an asset of political value to the government.

Canada was able to join a coalition that had taken form at the CCW review conference in Geneva in 1995-6. This coalition developed as some participants came to the conclusion that the negotiations within the Conference on Disarmament could not move above the "lowest common denominator." Beyond the state-actors, a broadly based coalition of NGOs and the highly effective ICRC had developed political support for an APL ban in all regions. Canada's financial resources were limited, especially in 1996 when "program review" cut deeply into departmental budgets. The ICRC, fortunately, had an international presence and a willingness to commit its funds to conferences, television advertisements, and studies. The ICBL drew upon American foundations, traditional peace groups, and even the American government. In the case of the land mine initiative, Canada took the lead in a coalition that others had formed.

Why Canada? Delvoie urges that initiatives must be based "on a clear headed assessment of Canada's relative influence" and that the government "must have available a reservoir of relevant diplomatic and technical expertise." "Diplomatic credit" is also important in the assessment of whether an initiative should proceed. Here there is some debate and doubt. Some suggest that Canada "ran down" its "diplomatic credit" through the land mine campaign. Others question whether the effort strained the limits of Canada's diplomatic expertise at a time when the impact of program review required major restructuring of DFAIT. As embassies, ambassadors, and politicians twisted arms and paid for cocktails in order to gain signatories for the Ottawa Treaty, other concerns were ignored.[19]

It is probably too soon to judge whether Canada's "diplomatic credit" was depleted. Nevertheless, one can suggest that the land mine initiative built upon a traditional area of Canadian activity and concern. The arms control and disarmament division of DFAIT benefited from the presence of officers who had served in the division for many years. Indeed, the fact that normal rules of rotation in the division had not applied meant that officers were experienced and well prepared when the land mine campaign landed on their desks. Because of their knowledge of other foreign ministries, they were able to draw in other expertise on arms control to assist in creating the so-called "Ottawa Process." Thus, Austrian officials drafted the treaty while Belgium and Norway offered resources for the negotiations. The creation of a coalition, the "core group," was so successful that, after the Ottawa Treaty was signed, one European diplomat said in a forum on the Ottawa process that he had come to feel closer to the "core group" than to his own country.

This diplomat's comments suggest that Canada gained at least some "diplomatic credit" through the Ottawa Process, a perception that was strengthened in the spring of 1998 when Canada sent envoys to lobby for votes for a seat on the UN Security Council. In a broader sense, the land mine debate does raise the question of Canada's "relative influence." Andrew Cooper's discussion of "niche diplomacy" points out that Canada's diplomacy traditionally "has been characterized by its variety and diversification" but has favoured a "low-key, consensus-oriented style," unlike the more "heroic" or "initiative-oriented" Australians.[20] The land mine initiative and others in the post-Cold War era suggest, perhaps, that Canada is becoming more "heroic" as its ability to act across the broad policy spectrum is becoming more limited.

While Canada came late to the land mine campaign, it nevertheless fit into the leadership position with remarkable ease and acceptance. With the major powers dithering or at the side, smaller countries such as Belgium, Austria, Sweden, the Philippines, and South Africa pushed the campaign forward. Belgium, some Canadian officials reportedly thought in October 1996, might seize hold of the initiative if Canada did not. When Jody Williams heard this suggestion, she remarked that Belgium could never have taken the lead. In the land mine campaign, she argued, Canada's resources and relative influence were the most impressive. There was no other choice.[21] What might seem limitations in other respects became advantages in the land mine campaign. Canada does not have the extensive diplomatic presence of the Security Council members, but it is represented well on all continents, unlike other second-tier countries. Australia, for example, has largely withdrawn from Africa and is minimally represented in the western hemisphere. Smaller European states such as Belgium are hindered by the restrictions of EU foreign policy. Moreover, Canada is much wealthier than states with larger populations in the second tier, such as the Philippines or South Africa, while possessing greater diplomatic resources than smaller wealthy states such as Sweden, Norway, and Belgium that were "heroic" actors in the past. These considerations suggest that Canada may find itself the "chosen" for future initiatives. But to what end?

The Canadians' performance, critics said, was "miserable," an act of "desertion," "woolly," and indifferent to "the power aspect." These comments were made in 1956 about Pearson's Suez initiative by, respectively, Britain's prime minister, Anthony Eden; senior Canadian diplomat Charles Ritchie; and Dean Acheson. And yet Kim Nossal identifies Suez as transformative, the triumph that others crave. In 1956, however, it was much less popular in Canada than the Axworthy initiative. In the House of Commons, Pearson faced strong censure from the Conservative Opposition for his abandonment of Great Britain. In External Affairs, Charles Ritchie complained that Canada was being too influenced "by unreal majorities of the United Nations" and was forgetting that Britain was "the best bet in a bad world." [22] Pearson, nevertheless, won the Nobel Prize for his efforts. Jody Williams and the ICBL, not Lloyd Axworthy, received the Nobel Prize for theirs two generations later. The choice and the comparison says much about how Canada, the world, and diplomacy have changed. "Serious foreign policy" has become entangled in a complex tissue of NGOs, international organizations, media with global reach, and the traditional distinctions of *Aussenpolitik* and *Innenpolitik*, so fundamental to the scholarship and practice of diplomacy, have lost meaning. For Canada, however, their meaning was always elusive.

For Canada, a diverse and often divided country in which identity itself seems elusive, some things do remain the same. Canada never had land mines on its borders; its soldiers last used them in

Korea; and it had not even bothered to ratify the amended Land mine Protocol more than a decade after its negotiation. As others raised their voices at the beginning of the 1990s, Canada nodded in agreement but usually did not speak. Yet, taken by the swelling flood of concern in the mid-1990s, Canada was swept forward towards its greatest foreign-policy success in decades. "It was," one might say again, "largely a question of sentiment." To condemn the land mine campaign as "emotional" misses the point. For Canada and increasingly for others, emotion matters, and recognition is a treasured coin of the realm.

NOTES

1   Henry Kissinger quoted in Frank Ninkovich, "No Post-Mortems for Postmodernism, Please," *Diplomatic History,* vol 22 (summer 1998), 463.

2   Henry Borden, ed., *Robert Laird Borden: His Memoirs* (London: Macmillan, 1938), 899.

3   W.A. Riddell, *World Security by Conference* (Toronto: Ryerson Press, 1947), 1.

4   Borden was rated seventh overall and a "high-average" prime minister by the panel of historians. Norman Hillmer and J.L. Granatstein, "Historians Rank the Best and Worst Canadian Prime Ministers," *Maclean's,* <http://www.macleans.ca/news-room04219// spc04219/.html>, 27 April 1997.

5   *Globe and Mail,* 11 July 1998.

6   Dean Acheson, "Canada: 'Stern Daughter of the Voice of God,'" in Livingston Merchant, ed., *Neighbors Taken for Granted: Canada and the United States* (New York: Publisher for the School of Adjoined International Studies, The John Hopkins University, 1966), 134-41.

7   American Embassy, Ottawa, to Dept. of State, 6 May 1962, State Dept. Records 742.00/5-862. I would like to thank Professor Denis Smith for this reference. Pearson is said to be "sophisticated and experienced in world affairs," but it was suggested that he would not necessarily be more sympathetic to basic American policy.

8   Henry Kissinger, *White House Years* (Boston: Little Brown, 1979), 383.

9   Ottawa *Citizen*, 6 July 1998.

10 David Lenarcic, *Knight-Errant? Canada and the Crusade to Ban Anti-Personnel Land Mines* (Toronto: Irwin Publishing Ltd., 1998); Dean Oliver, "Mine Treaty Simplistic and Emotion," Ottawa *Citizen*, 1 October 1997; and "Editorial," *Peacekeeping and International Relations* (January-February 1998), 1-2.

11 ICRC, *Anti-personnel Landmines: Friend or Foe?* (Geneva: ICRC, 1996), 73; and ICRC, *Landmines Must Be Stopped* (Geneva: ICRC, 1995).

12 Brian Tomlin, "On a Fast-Track to a Ban: The Canadian Policy Process," *Canadian Foreign Policy* (forthcoming). See also, Robert Lawson, "The Ottawa Process: Fast-Track Diplomacy and the International Movement to Ban Anti-Personnel Mines," in Fen Osler Hampson and Maureen Appel Molot, eds., *Canada Among Nations 1998: Leadership and Dialogue* (Toronto: Oxford University Press, 1998), 80-98.

13 Boutros Boutros-Ghali, "The Land Mine Crisis: A Humanitarian Disaster," *Foreign Affairs*, vol 73 (September-October 1994), 8-13. For a fuller account of this background, see John English, "The Ottawa Process: Paths Followed, Paths Ahead," *Australian Journal of International Affairs* 52 (July 1998), 121–132.

14 Thomas McNamara, "The U.S. Approach Toward Land Mines: A Realistic Policy for an Evolving Problem," in Kevin Cahill, ed., *Clearing the Fields: Solutions to the Global Land Mines Crisis* (New York: Basic Books and the Council on Foreign Relations, 1995), 61.

15 United States Department of State. *Hidden Killers: The Global Problem with Uncleared Landmines* (Washington, D.C.:A Report on International De-mining, 1993), 2.

16 Cyrus Vance and Herbert Okun, "Eliminating the Threat of Land Mines: A New US Policy," in Cahill, ed., *Clearing the Fields*, 204.

17 Comments of General Robert Gard at Ottawa Process Forum, 5 December 1997.

18 The quotation is from Tomlin, "On a Fast-Track to a Ban." See also Lawson, "The Ottawa Process."

19 John Carson of the University of Toronto told a reporter that "although there is nothing dilettantish about getting rid of

land-mines and setting up a permanent militarized unit for the United Nations and other things that our foreign minister backs occasionally, these are the kinds of things which are described as dilettantish because they tend to be issues that look a lot better than the weight of their substance.' Ottawa *Citizen*, 6 July 1998.

[20] Andrew Cooper, "Niche Diplomacy: A Conceptual Overview," in Andrew Cooper, ed., *Niche Diplomacy: Middle Powers after the Cold War* (New York: St. Martin's Press, 1997), 1-24.

[21] Comments made in discussions at Carleton University, 6 March 1998.

[22] John English, *The Worldly Years: The Life of Lester Pearson 1949-1972* (Toronto: Vintage Books, 1993), 141-3

Chapter Four

Mission Impossible: Canadian Diplomatic Initiatives from Mines to Markets

Claire Turenne Sjolander and Miguel de Larrinaga

> I speak for my own government, and others as well, to tell you that ... we have used all the tools of international diplomacy—bilateral meetings and negotiations, démarche by ambassadors, phone calls by the Prime Minister to his counterparts—to produce the text of the convention and to build support for it within the community of nations.[1]

> In this day and age, no government—especially Canada's—can ignore the consequences of globalization. Quite the contrary, Canada can and must take advantage of the tremendous opportunity offered by a world without borders .... That is ... why the Prime Minister has led Team Canada missions to Asia and Latin America over the past ... years.[2]

At first glance, it would appear difficult, if not impossible, to compare the processes underlying the Canadian state's diplomatic initiative with respect to the banning of anti-personnel mines, and the "Team Canada" missions which try to position Canadian firms at the cutting edge of the global marketplace. The land mines initiative, leading to the December 1997 signing of the Ottawa Treaty (formally known as the Convention on the Stockpiling, Use, Transfer and Production of Land mines), was heralded as a significant breakthrough in the staid world of international diplomacy. An existing weapon of war was declared illegal by well over 100 states, and although many governments refused to sign the treaty, the rapidity with which an international coalition between states and civil society actors had been formed and had proven effective was proclaimed as a new model for multilateral diplomacy, a new recipe for the twenty-first century. Within this process, the Canadian state was attributed, and claimed, a leadership role. In contrast, the annual Team Canada trade- and investment-promotion pilgrimages to the warmer climes of Latin America and south and southeast Asia are designed to assist small and medium-sized Canadian firms to share in the prosperity of the world's most dynamic economies. Far from the idealistic vision of international humanitarian cooperation embodied in the land mines initiative, Team Canada responds to the hard, rationalist, business logic that imbues globalization. While the land mines initiative showcases the triumph of the human spirit at its finest hour, Team Canada missions are a technical response to the exigencies of the competitive and efficiency rationales of the global marketplace.

The conception of these two examples of mission diplomacy as quite distinct, and thus difficult to compare, is based upon accepting a particular vantage point: that of the state. In positing such a vantage point, the state assumes an a priori position from which these initiatives are given meaning.[3] However, if we reject an inherent, ontologically prior, position for the state,[4] the land mines initiative and Team Canada missions appear strikingly similar. Rather than accepting the state as a prior given, the state is itself shaped by the discourses and practices in which it participates. In rejecting a vantage point from the state, both cases reveal the way in which the state and specific world orders are mutually constituted, as well as how this construction enables the state to distance itself from its participation in the shaping of world order, an order for which it bears particular responsibility. In the case of land mines, the state is able to distance itself completely from its responsibility for the production and use of land mines and for the perpetuation of a global order that legitimates conflict. Through Team Canada missions, the state is able to distance itself from its responsibility in constructing and expanding an economic system in which social dislocation has become an increasingly prevalent feature. In successfully eschewing its responsibility in both instances, the state is able to define a new role, to construct a new activist diplomacy, and to portray itself as the champion of civil society in the face of external challenges. The land mines initiative defines a renewed advocacy role for middle powers, emphasizing persuasion rather than coercion, a post-Cold War "soft power" remedy that Canada is "ideally positioned" to exercise, rather than the blunt, hard, instruments of Cold War order.[5] Team Canada missions define the Canadian state's role as that of a facilitator—a novel diplomatic task encouraging "Canadian business ... to work with us in seizing the wealth of opportunity emerging in the global ... economy."[6] New partnerships are forged with civil-society actors as the new causes are embraced: humanitarian and development non-governmental initiatives (NGOs) in the case of the land mines initiative, and the Canadian business community with respect to Team Canada.

The question of this chapter, then, becomes one of how the state was able to side-step its responsibility and position itself in both cases as a supporter of civil society despite its participation in the shaping of the world order which gave rise to these problems. The answer is to be found in the way in which both the land mines initiative and Team Canada missions have been framed discursively. In both of these cases, particular dichotomies enable the "de-responsibilization" of the state through a depoliticization of the issue. For land mines, the central dichotomy permitting this depoliticization is articulated in the contrast between human and machine. The machine is the land mine, and the mine itself thus becomes the enemy preying on its innocent human victims. The mine/machine becomes the "other" from which a diplomatic consensus between states, and a new consensus between states and civil society, can be forged. For Team Canada, the central dichotomy operating is one of politics versus economics. Team Canada missions are seen as a necessary response to a globalizing economy, as permissible—and required—state interventions in the non-political realm of international economics. In responding to this economic "other," the state is able to paint globalization as an inevitable process from which there is no escape, and the social dislocations that may result are a necessary, if unfortunate, evil. Given the limited room for manoeuvre that globalization "imposes," Team Canada missions become the state's response to the challenge of fostering a more competitive—and job producing—marketplace, a possible cure for the nefarious effects of a restructuring global economy. From the state's perspective, while there is a clear political commitment involved in pursuing the land mines initiative, Team Canada is but a choice among technical options, im-

39

posed in the first instance by external economic "realities." By contrast, refusing to adopt a position from the vantage point of the state makes clear that the state inserts itself within a discourse articulated around dichotomies which serve to depoliticize its role, both in the production and use of land mines and in the structuring of the processes of globalization.

From Mines ...

In order to understand how the state was able to distance itself from any responsibility for the production and use of land mines, it is crucial to understand how land mines were "reinterpreted" from a legitimate weapon of war in the arsenals of sovereign states to an illegitimate "enemy" lying in wait for its human victims. At the outset of the international campaign mobilized by NGOs in support of a ban on anti-personnel mines, most state militaries—including Canada's—argued in favour of retaining access to mines as a necessary and indispensable instrument of war.[7] Counterposed to this interpretation of land mines as a weapon whose use could be justified militarily, given the right and responsibility of sovereign states to defend their populations in times of conflict, civil-society actors ranging from the International Committee of the Red Cross, the International Campaign to Ban Land mines, and, in Canada, Mines Action Canada, emphasized the humanitarian toll that land mines exacted. The military utility of land mines, they argued, could not be justified given the high price that was being paid by non-combatants around the world, often for years after open hostilities had ended. This change in the understanding of land mines is significant. Mines go from being an instrument *used* by states to protect their populations, to agent-less weapons which by their very nature have a disproportionate impact on civilians.

The lengthy process in the evolution of the framing of the land mines issue from one of military utility to one of mines as a humanitarian scourge posed a potential problem for the state. Quite simply, as long as mines were understood in terms of a debate over their military utility, states had something to say—in fact, they had the primary role in shaping the international discussion over land mines and their use. Such was indeed the case throughout the early 1990s, as states attempted to negotiate limits on the use of land mines within in the context of the Convention on Certain Conventional Weapons (CCW). As long as international negotiations were focused on the issue of the military utility of land mines, they could never achieve the objectives for a total ban championed by the NGO activists. In essence, fundamentally irreconcilable positions were being expressed; for states, the question revolved around whether and when land mine use can be justified, whereas for the NGO community, land mines had to be understood as a menace against humanity viewed through the prism of humanitarian law.

It is within the context of these irreconcilable positions that the Canadian state's diplomatic initiative on land mines has to be understood. As Bob Lawson, one of the diplomats involved in the land mines issue, has described, by January 1996, parallel to the deadlocked CCW process, "Canadian officials ... began to attend discrete meetings ... with NGO representatives and other pro-ban states to explore the potential for opening a new track of diplomatic action on the AP mine issue."[8] These meetings to define an alternative diplomatic avenue attempt, in many respects, to square the circle. Moving out of the CCW process, the humanitarian understanding of land mines becomes the terrain upon which new negotiations can take place. Because the state is the traditional "user" of land mines, however, the only way it can insert itself into this humanitarian terrain is to dissociate itself from its traditional role. Land mines as the agent-less enemy is the conceptual space that enables the state/civil society partnership to develop and thereby creates the possibility for the state to reassume its leadership role on questions relating to land mines. Nowhere is this illustrated more starkly than in Lloyd Axworthy's call to the community of states and NGOs to convene in Ottawa in December 1997 in order to sign an international agreement banning land mines. While Axworthy had been struck by the commitment of the "foreign officials and international aid workers" who had attended a land mine conference in Ottawa in October 1996, he was concerned that such energy and commitment would dissipate because "there was no logical next step to unlock the energies there."[9] The logical next step, for Axworthy and thus for the Canadian state, was to convene a state-led process on the conceptual terrain mapped out by the NGO activists; states could ban land mines because their military utility was not the issue—the mines themselves were. Speaking to his call for an international ban treaty, Axworthy argued, "It is at its core a simple matter. We cannot allow negotiations to fall into traditional habits and approaches. These are not strategic weapons ... It is a humanitarian issue. These weapons kill daily."[10]

Although land mines had been produced in Canada until 1992, mines were now constructed as an enemy "out there" from which humanity needed to be protected and for whose eradication the Canadian state would lead an international crusade. Land mines have been found guilty by the court of international diplomacy; it is the scourge or epidemic of mines from which "no member of our global society can be immune,"[11] and it is mines that have maimed and killed, rather than those who laid them. Prime Minister Jean Chrétien's speech on the occasion of the treaty-signing conference in December 1997 makes reference to mines as "murderers," "killing machines," as purveyors of destruction and slaughter[12]—mines are the animate objects that have visited horror and terror upon an unsuspecting civil society. The responsibility borne by states, for such responsibility does exist, is a "renewed sense of responsibility" which comes from the knowledge that "there are still millions of anti-personnel mines in the ground" which must be cleared.[13] This renewed responsibility has nothing to do with the role states have played in sanctioning or participating in a world order in which the stockpiling, use, transfer, and production of land mines is a frightening by-product. On this, the Canadian state's land mines initiative stands silent.

... To Markets

The first Team Canada trade-promotion mission was launched in November 1994. The prime minister, together with nine provincial premiers (Quebec's Jacques Parizeau did not participate), various cabinet ministers, and roughly 400 business leaders set out to the Far East to promote Canadian trade and investment opportunities and to conclude business deals in China, Hong Kong, Indonesia, and Vietnam. Conceived as the high-profile "tip" of an international business development "iceberg" designed to respond to the need to "promote jobs, growth and prosperity,"[14] Team Canada missions were developed as a strategic response to the exigencies of a globalizing marketplace. Just as the "human versus machine" dichotomy enabled the Canadian state to define a leadership role for itself within the context of the NGO-driven land mines initiative, so did a similar dichotomy between economics and politics enable the construction of a facilitator role for the Canadian state within the context of globalization. This role, we argue, is best expressed in the Team Canada concept. Globalization, represented as the dismantling of barriers, is an undeniable reality—a fact. As Jean Chrétien explained to his counterparts at the Santiago Summit: "My colleagues, let us tell our people—let us tell the world loud and clear, once and for all—that as we turn the page to a new century, the era of building walls is over ... In my country, we know that. This is not an economic theory. It is an economic fact."[15]

Within the "factual" context of globalization, trade and investment promotion becomes a technical problem, whose success can be measured by the dollar value of the "deals" that are concluded. The logic underscoring Team Canada missions is simple and irrefutable—because it is not defined in political terms: "For Canadian companies, [Team Canada missions] ... mean new markets and increased sales. For Canada, they mean jobs."[16] As Sergio Marchi argued in February 1998, "you might say that as International Trade Minister, I am Canada's 'minister in charge of deals'... Through trade missions like our very successful Team Canada trips ... my job really comes down to one thing: Helping Canadian business—and through them the Canadian public—get the best possible deals."[17] The role of the Canadian state is to help, to facilitate, to assist Canadian firms to position themselves in the global economy. In order to accomplish this task, "Team Canada Inc." provides the required technical assistance. It is an elaborate inter-departmental, inter-governmental network founded on a partnership with the Canadian business community. It includes the establishment of a Team Canada Inc. advisory board, a 30 per cent increase in the number of trade commissioners posted overseas, a new unit in the Department of Foreign Affairs and International Trade (DFAIT) to focus on the export needs of small- and medium-sized enterprises (SMEs), a web site, and a 24-hour toll-free number. "All levels of government and the private sector must work together as partners to *encourage* and *assist* Canadian companies—particularly... SMEs—in selling their products and services around the world."[18]

This characterization of the role of the Canadian state does not question why some Canadian firms require encouragement and assistance in the first place. The global context into which Canadian firms must integrate themselves, or else Canadian jobs, growth and prosperity are put in doubt, is itself not questioned; it is simply a given. Through its deeds, however, the Canadian state actively participates in creating that global context and in promoting a particular vision of globalization, but the context and the vision are ones in which the Canadian state, and Canadian firms, are portrayed as players on a stage that is not of their own making. Globalization is "out there," creating circumstances that must be confronted. Failure to do so brings with it dire consequences: "Are Canadians prepared to accept the decline in our standard of living that would be sure to result from trying to hide from globalization?"[19]

Represented as business responses to business problems, Team Canada missions, however, contribute to the creation and maintenance of globalization, both as a series of practices and as a set of ideas. They are part of the fabric of globalization, despite—and because of—their portrayal as an answer to globalization, of thus being somehow "outside" of it. Put forward as a technical response designed to create jobs and open new markets, Team Canada missions and the discourse surrounding them actively contribute to the reification of the politics/economics dichotomy that is central to globalization. In situating itself on a terrain that is defined as inherently non-political, Team Canada contributes to the understanding of globalization in non-political terms—as an incontrovertible economic reality. As a trade- and investment-promotion strategy, however, Team Canada is predicated upon continued economic liberalization; it makes "sense" only as a technical response to globalization if, at the same time, the Canadian state is actively engaged in promoting trade and investment liberalization in multilateral and bilateral fora in order to further the march of globalization. What is profoundly political is thus cast as somehow beyond politics.

The extent to which globalization and the state's responses to it are seen as beyond politics is particularly telling. In reaction to protests against international trade and investment negotiations (the necessary backdrop to Team Canada diplomacy), Sergio Marchi railed against "some groups" which "are criticizing" potential agreements (in this context, the Multilateral Agreement on Investment), "using" them to "attack free trade, globalization, [and] open borders." Marchi went on to argue that "we have to listen to these voices but we must also weigh them against the Canadian reality."[20] The dichotomy between politics and economics here is evident and is revealed in two ways. First, international negotiations promoting trade and investment liberalization are seen as distinct from globalization—as political negotiations, they are outside the somehow autonomous economic realm of free trade, globalization, and open borders. The fact that such negotiations produce agreements which structure the processes of globalization is not acknowledged in Marchi's invocation. Second, while civil-society actors engaged in *political* protest must be listened to, their voices need to be weighed against the hard facts of the *economic* bottom line—the indisputable reality of globalization. In contrast to the links forged with "protesting" (and political) NGOs in the land mines initiatives, such groups are given short shrift here. The state-society links forged in this case are those with a community that does not often define its bread-and-butter activities in political terms—business, and its corollary, hard-working Canadians looking for jobs, training for jobs, or trying to protect their jobs.

In promoting the idea that Team Canada is outside the realm of politics, a novel "diplomatic" role for the Canadian state is thus forged. Team Canada missions do not reflect the characterization of globalization as a set of processes contributing to the erosion of state sovereignty and the limitation of political room for manoeuvre. They do not do so because they are not understood as political. Rather, Team Canada missions situate themselves on a terrain in which the economic is completely separate from the political, and where the state can be seen to be attempting to harness the dynamism of the global economy—although not shaping it. On the Canadian state's role in the construction of that very same global economy, and thus its responsibility for some of its more deleterious consequences, Team Canada's silence speaks eloquently.

Conclusion

We began this chapter by pointing to the apparent difficulty, if not the impossibility, of a comparison between two so seemingly different diplomatic initiatives as land mines and Team Canada—the authors' own "mission impossible." In fact, however, it is in the possibility of a comparison between these two examples of "diplomatic missions" that another meaning to "impossible" is revealed. "Mission impossible" is found in the impossibility of a state mission—impossible in the sense that, in positing no ontological status to the state, the approach used in this chapter reveals the extent to which "state" missions, in the sense of the state as an agent acting independently upon a world "out there," are inherently "impossible." In rejecting the vantage point of the state, this chapter reveals the extent to which both the land mines initiative and Team Canada represent the eschewing of the state's traditional diplomatic role—an explicitly political one. In both cases, the Canadian state is able to distance itself from the responsibility traditionally shouldered by states with regards to *raison d'état*. It is through the depoliticization of issues surrounding both land mines and Team Canada that the state is able to forge partnerships with different segments of civil society, portraying itself as promoting an activist diplomacy (where the real "activity" is to be found in the process of depoliticization) and thus creating the possibility of a new "mission diplomacy." In so doing, the impossibility of traditional diplomatic missions in the construction of a globalizing post-Cold War world is revealed.

NOTES

1   Department of Foreign Affairs and International Trade, (hereafter DFAIT) "An Address by the Honourable Lloyd Axworthy, Minister of Foreign Affairs, to the Opening of the Mine Action Forum," Ottawa, 2 December 1997, 3.

2   Lloyd Axworthy, "Between Globalization and Multipolarity: The Case for a Global, Humane Canadian Foreign Policy," Ottawa,

DFAIT, <http://www.dfait-maeci.gc.ca/english/foreign/humane.htm>, December 1996.

3   For a more detailed theoretical discussion of the implications of assuming, and rejecting, an ontologically prior position for the state (discussed in terms of the relationship between the state and civil society), see Miguel de Larrinaga and Claire Turenne Sjolander, "(Re)presenting Land Mines from Protector to Enemy: Discursive Framing of a New Multilateralism," *Canadian Foreign Policy* 5/3 (spring 1998). Some of the analysis of the land mines initiative presented here is drawn from this earlier article.

4   Assuming that the state has no ontologically prior position reveals the way in which the state must define itself by reference to what it is not. What the state *is* manifests itself through the discourse and practices in which it participates.

5   Lloyd Axworthy, "Between Globalization and Multipolarity."

6   DFAIT, "Marchi Announces Team Canada Inc.," <http://www.dfait-maeci.gc.ca/english/news/ press_1/97_press/ 97_158E.HTM)>, 6 October 1997.

7   D'Arcy Jenish, "Landing the Prize: Peace Activists share in the 1997 Nobel," *Maclean's* 20 October 1997, 32.

8   Bob Lawson, "Towards a New Multilateralism: Canada and the Landmine Ban," *Behind the Headlines*, 54/4 (summer 1997), 20. The CCW process was deadlocked in terms of its ability to respond to growing NGO demands for a total ban.

9   Bruce Wallace, "The Battle to Ban Land Mines," *Maclean's*, 1 July 1997, 34.

10   DFAIT, "Notes for an Address by the Honourable Lloyd Axworthy Minister of Foreign Affairs at the Closing Session of the International Strategy Conference towards a Global Ban on Anti-Personnel Mines," Ottawa, <http://www.dfaitmaeci.gc.ca/english/news/statem 1/ 96_state/96_041e.htm, 5 October 1996.

11   Mark Moher, "Toward a Landmine Free Africa: The OAU and the Legacy of Anti-Personnel Mines," "Opening Plenary Statement by the Canadian Permanent Representative and Ambassador to the United Nations for Disarmament," Kempton Park, South Africa, 19 May 1997, 2.

47

12 Office of the Prime Minister, Canada, "Notes for an Address by Prime Minister Jean Chrétien on the occasion of the Treaty-Signing Conference of the Global Ban on Anti-Personnel Landmines," Ottawa, 3 December 1997.

13 DFAIT, "An Address by the Honourable Lloyd Axworthy, Minister of Foreign Affairs, to the Opening of the Mine Action Forum," 3-4.

14 DFAIT, *Opening Doors to the World: Canada's International Market Access Priorities 1998,* <http://www.infoexport.gc.ca/section4/mktx-e.asp>, 15 April 1998.

15 Office of the Prime Minister, Canada, "Notes for an Address by Prime Minister Jean Chrétien on the Occasion of the Closing Ceremony of the Second Summit of the Americas," Santiago, Chile, April 1998.

16 DFAIT, "Opening the Doors," *Info Export: On the road to exporting,* <http://www.infoexport.gc.ca/team_canada/supplement/latin1-e.htm>.

17 DFAIT, "Notes for an Address by the Honourable Sergio Marchi, Minister for International Trade, to the Centre for Trade Policy and Law," Ottawa, <http://www.dfaitmaeci.gc.ca/english/news/statement/98_state/98_008e.htm>, 13 February 1998.

18 DFAIT, "Marchi Announces Team Canada Inc." Emphasis added.

19 DFAIT, "Notes for an Address by the Honourable Sergio Marchi, Minister for International Trade, to the Centre for Trade Policy and Law."

20 DFAIT, "Notes for an Address by the Honourable Sergio Marchi, Minister for International Trade, to the Standing Committee on Foreign Affairs and International Trade: 'The Multilateral Agreement on Investment,'" Ottawa, <http://www.dfaitmaeci.gc.ca/english/news/statem1/97_state/97_048e.htm>, 4 November 1997.

Chapter Five

Canada, the Commonwealth, and Nigeria: The Limits of Ethical Multilateralism

David Black

When the Nigerian military regime provoked international outrage by executing Ken Saro-Wiwa and eight other Ogoni activists in November 1995, Canadian foreign policy makers attempted to take on a leadership role in the international effort to restore democracy, human rights, and the rule of law in that country. They advocated a combination of pressure and dialogue, with emphasis on the need for forceful punitive action. Their principal vehicle in this effort was the Commonwealth. Notwithstanding an intensive diplomatic effort both within this organization and beyond it, however, results fell considerably short of the government's initial objectives. In the two years between the beginning of the Commonwealth effort to promote change at the Auckland Commonwealth Heads of Government Meeting (CHOGM) in 1995 and the Edinburgh CHOGM of 1997, when the expulsion of Nigeria was threatened, the best that could be achieved was an agreement to maintain the country's suspension—well short of even the limited punitive measures favoured by Canada.

It could have been worse. Mid-way between the Auckland and Edinburgh CHOGMs, Canadian policy makers looked increasingly isolated in their "hard line" stand and the prospects for a credible Commonwealth consensus seemed slim. In the eight months prior to Edinburgh, a consensus was forged which rescued the organization's credibility and, more important, held out the prospect of additional pressure on the Nigerian regime if it failed to move decisively towards the entrenchment of democracy and human rights in its own putative transition, scheduled for completion by October 1998. Thus, the results of Canadian leadership in this area remain ambiguous and inconclusive.

Clearly, however, the government's Nigeria policy is a fine example of Canadian mission diplomacy, in the sense of an energetic attempt to do good in the world. And like other instances of mission diplomacy, this one was hampered, initially at least, by an inflated sense of our own influence and the willingness of others to follow our lead.

To understand both the potential significance and the real limitations of this ambiguous outcome, it is necessary first to assess the distinctive characteristics, opportunities, and limitations of the Commonwealth as a vehicle for human-rights activism, or ethical multilateralism. The fact that a particular institutional setting—the Commonwealth—was the principle vehicle for Canada's Nigeria policy clearly influenced its character and limits. I will then briefly trace the trajectory of this Canadian initiative, from enthusiastic advocacy through mounting frustration to partial recovery. Finally, I will consider the strengths, weaknesses, and implications of this initiative.

The Importance of the Commonwealth Context

An assessment of Canada's response to General Sani Abacha's Nigeria[1] must begin by confronting the limited and eroding basis for Canadian influence in Africa generally and Nigeria specifically, through aid, trade, and trans-societal connections. Given this eroding basis for influence, why would the Chrétien government have attempted to take on a leadership role in the case of Nigeria? A number of factors, both historic and idiosyncratic, help to account for this decision, as discussed below. However, the Commonwealth context was crucial in providing both opportunity and impetus for the government's approach.

The Commonwealth is a peculiar artefact of British imperialism. It has survived the demise of the empire and emerged as a surprisingly vital association of 54 countries spanning most conventional global divisions of wealth, culture, and region. It has offered peculiar opportunities and assets for Canadian foreign-policy makers. It is also characterized, however, by an ongoing quest for relevance and by structural limitations which often result in an apparent failure to live up to its promise.

The Commonwealth offers a rare forum in which Canada is unambiguously important. It provides a context in which Canadian leadership does not seem out of place, however marginal the issue in question might seem to Canadian interests in other contexts. Indeed, it virtually demands a higher level of engagement with certain issues than Canadian governments would have otherwise undertaken. Examples include Rhodesia/Zimbabwe, South Africa, and, most recently, Nigeria.

More broadly, the Commonwealth has several key institutional strengths.[2] There is, of course, its diversity: only UN agencies are more diverse, and they tend to be much more rigid in their procedures and constrained by bloc politics. The Commonwealth, by contrast, has developed a more informal and flexible organizational culture. Moreover, its diversity gives its pronouncements and actions on certain issues a degree of moral authority out of proportion to its material weight. The best example in this regard remains its activism on South Africa during the 1980s.

Operationally, the Commonwealth has now institutionalized procedures for creating what amount to cross-cutting coalitions on key policy challenges. Thus, on southern Africa, Commonwealth efforts were spearheaded from 1987 onwards by the Canadian-chaired Committee of Foreign Ministers on Southern Africa (CFMSA), whose eight members included several regional powers and key states from Asia, Africa, Australasia, and the Caribbean. Similarly, on Nigeria, the Gambia, and Sierra Leone, leaders created the Commonwealth Ministerial Action Group (CMAG) at the Auckland CHOGM to "deal with serious or persistent violations of the principles contained in (the Harare) Declaration" pertaining to democracy, human rights, and the rule of law.[3] Such committees would appear to be quite formidable vehicles for consensus building on multilateral action; yet, in practice, they have struggled with differences arising from their very diversity and representivity.

The Commonwealth is also noted for relatively small-scale but often quite creative programs of technical and functional cooperation. Canada has consistently been one of the principal funders of these activities. Finally, beyond the intergovernmental Commonwealth, the role of the "informal Commonwealth" bears emphasis.

Numerous non-governmental forums, including associations of Commonwealth lawyers, journalists, and parliamentarians and the Commonwealth Human Rights Initiative (CHRI), can and have given the Commonwealth an active and constructive presence in many parts of the world. They have been prominent in the case of Nigeria. Thus, the Commonwealth has a number of strengths and a retinue of eloquent enthusiasts in various parts of the world. Its continued popularity is reflected in the fact that countries with only limited historical ties to the empire, such as Mozambique and Cameroon, are now seeking and obtaining membership.

The Commonwealth also faces an ongoing question of relevance, however. Ever since the economic glue of Commonwealth preferences and the interpersonal glue of a first generation of leaders largely schooled in the United Kingdom came unstuck in the late 1960s and early 1970s, its future has been uncertain. What core mission justifies the continued allocation of scarce resources to this organization? During the 1960s, 1970s, and 1980s, its central political mission was the struggle against minority rule in southern Africa. The demise of apartheid from 1990 coincided with a shift in Commonwealth leadership, with the flamboyant Sonny Ramphal being replaced as secretary general by the lower-key diplomatic veteran, Nigerian Emeka Anyaoku. Both the organization and the new secretary general thus faced the need to identify a new core mission. While the Commonwealth's contribution to the demise of apartheid has often been overstated, the organization nevertheless considered its principled stand on this issue to have been one of its finest moments. This historic consideration, combined with its limited ability to mobilize economic or strategic resources, made the promotion of "Commonwealth values" a logical new focus. These were rather unexceptionally defined in the organization's 1991 Harare Declaration as the promotion of democracy, "democratic processes and institutions which reflect national circumstances," fundamental human rights, the rule of law and judicial independence, and "just and honest government."

Having chosen to place these values at its constitutive core, the organization was confronted with the challenge of giving effect to this mission.[4] At one level, this was simple enough: where Commonwealth member states were already undertaking democratic transitions or attempting to strengthen their human-rights performance, constitutional and legal structures, and so on, the organization provided welcome advice, electoral assistance, technical expertise, training, and the like. However, it had considerably more difficulty in agreeing on how to deal with member states in violation of Harare Declaration principles. After all, many Commonwealth countries had dubious records on these principles and there was considerable disagreement on what they implied in practice. Indeed, it was not until the Auckland Summit, four years after Harare, that agreement was reached on guidelines for responding to such violators and embedded in the Millbrook Commonwealth Action Programme on the Harare Declaration.

With this background, it is clear why the organization and its members felt compelled to respond forcefully to the breathtaking provocation of the Abacha regime's execution of the Ogoni Nine, even as the Auckland Summit was under way. Certain key leaders were particularly moved: Jean Chrétien, for one, apparently distinguished himself by being the only leader to warn in his opening remarks that carrying out the sentence would clearly violate Harare principles. Nelson Mandela, for another, was deeply angered by the Nigerian government's flaunting of his government's "softly-softly" quiet diplomacy. The bold decision to suspend Nigeria, and to threaten it with expulsion if it did not bring its policies into line with Harare principles, was therefore predictable enough. Moreover, the Commonwealth now had an instrument at its disposal—the CMAG—for carrying forward its effort to promote change in Nigeria.

Yet, notwithstanding this bold stand, implying stronger measures to come, the Commonwealth's ability to act on this and other issues is structurally limited by its fundamentally marginal nature in relation to its members' core priorities. As Stephen Chan has noted, "every part of its membership ... is committed to its own regional organization ... or to particular power relationships which may militate against Commonwealth co-operation ... The Commonwealth internationally organises its membership only when other more major factors permit it to."[5] The Commonwealth's marginal foreign-policy significance to Canada is reflected in the fact that the Commonwealth

53

Affairs section of DFAIT's United Nations and Commonwealth Affairs Division has only two officers. In the case of CMAG, Canada and New Zealand took similarly strong positions and Jamaica tended to cooperate with these two Western members; Britain under John Major's Tories was less openly antagonistic to sanctions than Thatcher's Tories had been but was still consistent in its aversion to such measures; Malaysia was generally opposed to actions that would legitimate (further) intervention in the affairs of a sovereign state on human-rights grounds; Zimbabwe and South Africa found themselves much more constrained by norms of African solidarity than the latter, in particular, had anticipated; and Nigeria's ECOWAS[6] neighbour, Ghana, was especially vulnerable to Nigerian retribution in both economic and security terms. As with other matters of high political sensitivity in Commonwealth affairs, therefore, it proved extremely difficult to sustain a working consensus consistent with the organization's initial strong stand.

In addition, a Commonwealth concerned with maintaining its vitality and credibility was loathe to drive out Nigeria—Africa's most populous country and self-styled "great power." This consideration surely served as a brake on stronger punitive action.[7] It is significant, moreover, that despite taking great offence at the Commonwealth's "regrettable error" and "unjust" action in suspending it (in the words of Foreign Minister Tom Ikimi), the Nigerian government has not quit the organization, as apartheid South Africa did in 1961. Rather, it has lobbied fiercely for rehabilitation, albeit on its own terms. This indicates two things: that it still places considerable value on its Commonwealth membership; and that the suspension hurt. Even this limited act can therefore be considered to have been an effective diplomatic sanction.

Canada and CMAG, 1995-7: A Chronicle of Frustration and Partial Recovery

The Commonwealth was not the only vehicle for Canada's post-1995 Nigeria policy.[8] The government created a small two-year, $2.2-million Democratic Development Fund to support the efforts of Canadian and Nigerian non-governmental organizations (NGOs) to foster positive political change in Nigeria, as well as the Gambia and Sierra Leone. DFAIT also used its visits program to bring in Nigerian human-rights activists, to the great consternation of the Abacha regime. As early as 1993, following the annulment of the presidential elections of 12 June by Sani Abacha's predecessor, General Ibrahim Babangida, the government had implemented some symbolic punitive measures on a bilateral basis. In the wake of the 1995 executions, the House of Commons Standing Committee on Foreign Affairs and International Trade took up the Nigerian issue at hearings in December 1995 and June 1996, and advocated a "strong leadership role (for Canada) in co-ordinating an 'enforceable' oil embargo."[9] Multilaterally, Canadian representatives lobbied for resolutions on the human-rights situation in Nigeria at the UN General Assembly and the UN Commission on Human Rights. More significantly, in the latter, Canada supported the appointment of two special rapporteurs to investigate arbitrary executions and the independence of the judiciary respectively in 1996. When the efforts of these rapporteurs were blocked, it supported the stronger step of appointing a special-country rapporteur for Nigeria in April 1997.

Thus, Canadian policy moved on several complementary fronts; but it was the Commonwealth, and more particularly CMAG, which was its principal focus. There were no less than eight CMAG meetings and one ministerial mission to Nigeria during the two-year period between Auckland and Edinburgh. While the Gambia and Sierra Leone were also under scrutiny, the group's principal preoccupation was Nigeria. The CMAG process represented a major diplomatic commitment on the part of Canada and other member states. Canadian fortunes in this process can be divided into two phases: a period of mounting division within the group, and frustration and isolation for Canadian policy makers, extending through February 1997; and a period of partial recovery in which a more muted Commonwealth consensus was restored, partly through the efforts of Canadian officials.

In the first several months and couple of CMAG meetings, the Commonwealth consensus on a hard line seemed to hold. At the second, April 1996 meeting, Canada drove an agreement within the Group to recommend a package of limited sanctions measures, including visa restrictions on members of the Nigerian regime and their families, the withdrawal of military attachés, cessation of military training, an embargo on the export of arms, denial of educational facilities to members of the regime and their families, a ban on sporting contacts, and the downgrading of cultural links and diplomatic missions.[10] In these early months, South Africa was an important fellow traveller, as it continued to argue for strong punitive measures, setting off a bitter war of words between Africa's two strongest governments.[11] There were also early signs of trouble for the Canadian position, however, as la Francophonie was unable to agree on anything stronger than a toothless appeal to the Nigerian authorities for the establishment of the rule of law and democracy. Nigeria's west African neighbours were particularly and predictably reluctant to criticize the regime. In May 1996 the report of a UN fact-finding mission was released. While it criticized the human-rights situation and abuses of the rule of law in Nigeria, it also praised Abacha's "statesmanship" and "his willingness to be transparent" by inviting the mission and recommended against sanctions at that time.[12]

From its June meeting, at which CMAG representatives and a delegation from the Nigerian regime met face-to-face in London, most of the rest of the committee began to diverge from the Canadian position. Whereas CMAG as a whole recommended holding in reserve the measures recommended in April, Canada went ahead with its implementation and argued for additional sanctions pressure. By this time, the Nigerian regime had been stalling for months on one of CMAG's earliest decisions: to send a ministerial fact-finding mission to the country in a manner reminiscent of the influential "Mission to South Africa" of the Commonwealth's Eminent Persons Group (EPG) in the mid-1980s. A visit by four Commonwealth officials to Nigeria in September 1996 to try to facilitate this mission resulted in a major retreat on the Commonwealth's part concerning its scope and duration. This must have contributed to a particularly sharp exchange between Canadian Foreign Minister Lloyd Axworthy and an unnamed Commonwealth official around the Group's fifth meeting in New York at the end of September.[13]

By this time, too, erstwhile hard-line ally South Africa was retreating to a more conciliatory position. Canada-Nigeria relations had become frigid, as the Nigerian High Commission in Ottawa was closed and the Nigerians refused to cooperate in making alternative arrangements for consular services. When, after protracted negotiations, arrangements for a CMAG ministerial mission to Nigeria were finally set for 19-20 November 1996, Canadian Secretary of State for Africa and Latin America Christine Stewart felt compelled to withdraw when the Nigerian government refused to grant visas for two RCMP officers who were to accompany her. When the mission arrived in Nigeria, Nigerian Foreign Minister Tom Ikimi's opening remarks included an inflammatory attack on Canada's supposedly seditious activities in his country.

Why did the Canadian government maintain such a hard line on sanctions, particularly when it was advocating "working from within" (or "constructive engagement") in relation to other human-rights violators such as Indonesia, China, and Cuba? Its tough approach clearly resonated domestically.[14] It was particularly popular in light of widespread discomfiture over the Chrétien government's apparently amoral pursuit of trade opportunities at the expense of human-rights concerns in its early years in office. Evan Potter has argued that this domestic political impetus was reinforced by the arrival of Lloyd Axworthy as foreign minister shortly after the crisis had broken. Axworthy wanted to signal a shift towards a more "humane internationalist" foreign policy, and Nigeria presented a high-profile opportunity to send this signal.[15] The Canadian position was also arguably shaped in part by a misplaced analogy with the Commonwealth's earlier activism on South Africa and a mythologized conception of the importance of Canadian leadership in that earlier case. A widely held "common sense" view has developed in this country that, on South Africa, Canada had led and the Commonwealth followed.[16] In fact, Canada (and Australia) had come into line with the position that the Commonwealth majority had been advocating for some time. It is likely, therefore, that on Nigeria, Canadian political leaders reasoned from this mythologized view that the Commonwealth would once again follow a strong lead by Canada on this apparently similar issue. These misplaced expectations probably help to account for the frustration expressed by Axworthy towards the Commonwealth as it became clear that this was not occurring. In short, Canadian policy makers were not wrong to take a strong position on

57

Nigeria; however, they could have been better prepared for the predictable repercussions of their policy and pursued it with greater finesse in the Commonwealth context.

As it happened, Christine Stewart's withdrawal from the CMAG ministerial mission to Nigeria in November 1996 was the nadir of Canada's fortunes on this issue. From February onwards, the Group, mindful of the scrutiny its parent organization would face in Edinburgh, began to work back towards a consensus. Its extensive final report usefully reviewed its own activities as well as Nigeria's record of equivocation, manipulation, and continued human-rights abuses along the road to its putative 1 October 1998 "democratic" transition to civilian rule. In light of its relatively strong and critical assessment, CMAG concluded that Nigeria's suspension should be continued; that in the run-up to October 1998, the Group should be empowered to invoke the Commonwealth-wide implementation of some or all of the sanctions originally recommended in April 1996; and that if, in its assessment, Nigeria had not completed a credible democratic transition by 1 October 1998, it should then consider its expulsion and further sanctions measures "in consultation with other members of the international community." These would include a mandatory oil embargo, a ban on air links, and freezing the financial assets and foreign bank accounts of members of the regime and their families. In concrete terms, this conclusion (endorsed by heads of government at Edinburgh) added nothing to the steps already taken by the organization and continued to hold in abeyance stronger measures. Yet it also held out the threat of much stronger action to come should the transition fail to satisfy Harare Declaration principles. It was a stronger outcome than seemed possible mid-way through the CMAG cycle.

Several factors help to account for this shift back towards Canada's position. While some were fortuitous, a couple can be credited to Canadian initiatives. First, the Nigerian regime's refusal to allow the ministerial mission access to the range of people it wished to meet while in Nigeria, including jailed presidential victor Mashood Abiola, and its stage-managed series of meetings forced Group members to confront directly the inconsistencies and insincerity of its transition program. More recently, and deeply ironically, the Nigerian-dominated ECOWAS intervention to restore the democratically elected president of Sierra Leone, deposed in a 25 May 1997 coup, placed into stark relief the unacceptability of its own military regime. The intervention was endorsed by the Organization of African Unity (OAU), the UN Security Council, and the Commonwealth. It was very difficult for these organizations to support intervention in aid of democracy in Sierra Leone while failing to do so in Nigeria itself.

Third, the election of the Labour government in Britain precipitated a sharp shift in British foreign policy towards a more ethically based approach. British Foreign Secretary Robin Cook has been closely in tune with Lloyd Axworthy on a range of issues, Nigeria included. This change of government led to a shift in the balance of forces in CMAG, with Canada's pro-sanctions position gaining an important new ally. It has been argued that the threats of strong future action in the CMAG report would have been inconceivable had the Tories retained power.[17]

Fourth, the Group was significantly influenced by the presentations of a number of leading Nigerian and international NGOs at its seventh meeting in July 1997. These NGOs were virtually unanimous in their misgivings about the transition program and in their concerns over the erosion of the rule of law and the condition of human rights in Nigeria. Canadian representatives had been arguing for some months that the Group needed to hear from such organizations in order to develop a balanced assessment. Their ultimate success in this argument helped to produce a stronger report than would otherwise have been possible.

Finally, the Canadian delegation apparently made a direct contribution to the strength of CMAG's final report through a classic instance of careful advance preparation. For the Group's final meeting prior to Edinburgh in September 1997, the Commonwealth Secretariat had produced a thorough review of the Group's activities but no assessment of their implications. The Canadian delegation argued that the report needed to incorporate such an assessment and, having won this point, produced a strongly worded draft which it had prepared prior to the meeting. In the absence of an alternative, it got most of the language it had wanted in this section, and thus a relatively strong set of conclusions for heads of government. In these ways, then, Canadian representatives regained some lost ground, and contributed to an outcome in Edinburgh that rescued the organization's strained credibility, at least temporarily.

Conclusions and Implications

Many Nigerian and international human-rights activists expressed frustration during the Edinburgh CHOGM over the organization's lack of substantial new actions and its failure to follow through on the threat to expel Nigeria in the absence of substantial progress towards Harare Declaration principles. Indeed, there was a lowest-common denominator quality to the consensus achieved, which fell short of even the limited sanctions measures consistently advocated by Canadian representatives.

Still, the significance of the position adopted in Edinburgh should not be dismissed. It is clear that Nigeria's suspension from the Commonwealth has been painful to the regime. The renewal of this suspension prolonged the pain. Moreover, the threat to consider much stronger sanctions in the absence of a credible transition by 1 October 1998, though obviously cheap talk when made, was the strongest stand yet taken by any international organization at that time. The divisions within CMAG through the 1995-7 period suggest that it will have great difficulty following through with the strong sanctions measures mooted at Edinburgh. Nevertheless, the Commonwealth's stand served notice to the Abacha regime that it would face substantial international resistance to a transparently flawed transition. The Canadian government deserves its share of the credit for this outcome, limited though it is.

Several broader lessons are underscored by this case. First, successful initiatives generally depend on careful preparation, both intellectual and institutional, as well as a substantial presence on the ground. These resources are not accumulated quickly or cheaply. While it is hard to know precisely how Canadian policy makers might have altered their approach with more careful preparation, it is apparent that they were caught off guard by the predictable dissension and setbacks during CMAG's first year and by the Nigerian government's vigorous counter-attack.

A second, closely related lesson is that in coalition settings, particular care must be taken to nurture crucial relationships. A notable case in point in this instance was the relationship between Canada and South Africa. A strong axis between these two countries, combined with a more sensitive understanding on both their parts of the dilemmas faced by other African states, could have been very useful and influential. As it was, this opportunity was lost.

In addition, however, coalition-building must be seen in broader terms than has traditionally been the case. National and international NGOs are emerging as vital potential allies in leadership initiatives. In this connection, Canadian policy makers did well to recognize the potential value of representations from Nigerian and international NGOs and to push for their appearance before CMAG.

Finally, and more broadly, it may be that the most durable significance of this initiative for Canada and the Commonwealth will have less to do with Nigeria than with the longer-term educative process of deepening collective understanding of the meaning and salience of democracy and human rights. The June 1998 death of Sani Abacha has provided some new basis for optimism in Nigeria, yet a deeply flawed transition still appears probable as this is written. In this context, it is quite likely that the Commonwealth will fail to live up to its threat to impose and campaign for much stronger international sanctions. If this happens, critics will argue once again that it is a wasting asset. In the meantime, however, Commonwealth representatives will have scrutinized and struggled with what a genuine democratic transition would entail. This, combined with the organization's lower-profile activities in support of democracy and human rights, may contribute to the deepening of these norms and principles internationally, albeit in ways that are often indirect and hard to measure.

NOTES

1 General Abacha died suddenly in June 1998, opening the way for a fragile democratic transition process under his successor, General Abdusalam Abubakar. The transition, which unfolded after the completion of this chapter, culminated in Presidential elections on 27 February 1999 and the inauguration of a new civil-

ian regime under ex-General Olusegun Obasanjo on 29 May of that year. This modestly hopeful outcome serves as a useful reminder of the role of fortune in politics.

2   On Commonwealth strengths and limitations, see, for example, Stephen Chan, *The Commonwealth in World Politics* (London: Lester Crook, 1988); and James Mayall, "Democratizing the Commonwealth," *International Affairs* 74/2 (1998) 379–392.

3   "The Millbrook Commonwealth Action Programme on the Harare Declaration" (1995). For text, see *The Round Table* 337 (1996), 123-6.

4   For a fine discussion of this process and its implications, see Mayall, "Democratizing the Commonwealth."

5   Chan, *The Commonwealth in World Politics*, 67.

6   The sixteen-member Economic Community of West African States.

7   As did the fact that the secretary general was Nigerian and would be ineligible to retain his position if Nigeria were expelled. Thanks to Louis Delvoie for clarifying this point.

8   For a good discussion of this policy, see Evan Potter, "Nigeria and the Commonwealth: Explaining Canada's Hard-Line Approach to Sanctions, 1995-96," *The Round Table* 342 (1997) 205–230.

9   Potter, "Explaining Canada's Hard-Line Approach," 213.

10 For a detailed summary of the Group's work, see "Report of the Commonwealth Ministerial Action Group on the Harare Declaration (CMAG) to Commonwealth Heads of Government," Commonwealth Secretariat, September 1997 (hereafter CMAG Report).

11 See Maxi van Aardt, "A Foreign Policy to Die For: South Africa's Response to the Nigeria Crisis," *Africa Insight* 26 (2), 1996.

12 CMAG Report, annex X.

13 Paul Knox, "Axworthy lashes out at Nigeria 'appeasers,'" *Globe and Mail*, 26 September 1996.

14 See "Punishing Nigeria" (editorial), *Globe and Mail*, 28 June 1996.

15 Potter, "Explaining Canada's Hard-Line Approach," 217-18. On the "humane internationalist" tradition in Canadian foreign policy, see Cranford Pratt, "Humane Internationalism: Its Signifi-

cance and Variants," in Pratt, ed., *Internationalism Under Strain* (Toronto: University of Toronto Press, 1989).

16 For a good example of this interpretation, see Barbara Mc-Dougall, "Why keep the Commonwealth?" *Globe and Mail*, 14 November 1997.

17 Confidential interview with DFAIT officials, 7 November 1997.

63

Chapter Six

Between Will and Capabilities: Canada and the Zaire/Great Lakes Initiative

Andrew F. Cooper

The difficulty of niche selection in Canadian diplomacy is highlighted by a case study of the Zaire/Great Lakes initiative. At first glance, this mission appears to fit well with the peacekeeping/humanitarian orientation of Canada's international activities.[1] A closer look at the initiative, however, reveals the extent to which this episode exhibits the classic flaws inherent in a case of misplaced niche selection. To begin with, serious questions could be asked about whether the central African region was inside or outside Canada's geographic area of specialization. Although the advocates of the initiative played up the notion that Canada was under some specific obligation to act in this case because of Canada's long standing reputation and connections with the area, these claims could be criticized for being exaggerated and misleading. Secondly, the initial enthusiasm for the mission displayed by Prime Minister Jean Chrétien and some other state officials was not matched by the quantity and quality of resources which were (and could) be devoted to the initiative. Thirdly, the initiative demonstrates many of the tensions found in Canadian statecraft between attempts to build selective coalitions of the willing (based on mobilizing a multilayered constellation of actors on an issue-by-issue basis) and the traditional reliance on the structural capacity of Great Power allies and the United States more specifically. The United States may no longer be inclined to exercise its traditional form of comprehensive leadership in the context of the post-Cold War. But without its support, alternative attempts at coalition-building and issue-specific targeting are extremely difficult to implement.

Locating the Niche

The manner by which Canada selected the Zaire/Great Lakes issue for concerted action was in many ways at odds with a disciplined mode of niche selection. The impetus for action at the end of 1996 did not arise out of a detailed, strategic assessment of the complex situation in the region, with due consideration for what the Canadian government should focus on and what resources should be devoted to getting results. Although versions differ about what served as the primary catalyst for launching the Canadian-led initiative, the common thread among these interpretations is the personalistic and emotionally laden framing of the issue. One variation of this theme has a telephone conversation between Prime Minister Chrétien and his nephew, the Canadian ambassador to the United Nations, serving as the trigger. As the secretary general of the United Nation's special envoy, Raymond Chrétien had been assigned the difficult task of ameliorating the crisis in the central African region. His message to his uncle was that the international community must do something to deal with the situation as quickly as possible.[2] Another variation highlights the influence of the prime minister's wife, Aline Chrétien, in drawing her husband's attention to the apocalyptic reports from CNN about the refugee situation, as they were spending a quiet weekend at the Harrington Lake prime ministerial retreat.

To emphasize the personal and the private attributes of niche selection is not to devalue the sense of public importance associated with the Zaire/Great Lakes initiative. Symbolically, a quick and decisive response from Ottawa buttressed Canada's long-standing claim to be a committed and constructive global actor. From the outset, this sense of good international citizenship shaped the tone of Chrétien's declaratory statements. In a press conference held on 12 November 1996, the prime minister declared: "Canada may not be a superpower but we are a nation that speaks on the international scene with great moral authority ... now is the time to use that moral authority to stop suffering, avert disaster."[3]

More instrumentally, choosing to concentrate a good deal of will and resources in this sphere of activity could be linked to a number of potential political advantages for the Chrétien government. One of the prime ways in which the central African region took on definition as a geographical niche for Canadian activity was through the francophone construct. A key standard for evaluation of the initiative, therefore, was the way in which it was received by Quebec public opinion. The fact that this reception appeared, initially at least, to be positive lent the weight of some added domestic political credibility towards the endeavour.[4]

A demonstration of will expressed through this mission also provided a valuable means by which relations between the Liberal government and the nongovernmental (NGO) community could be rebuilt. Indeed, it was the call for help from societal groups loosely clustered around the Rwanda NGO executive committee that did much to prepare the way for governmental action. Organizations such as the Red Cross, Oxfam, Care Canada, and Doctors without Borders (all of which had extensive networks of field workers in central Africa) provided the refugee figures (estimated at 1.2 million) and gave weight to the sheer extent of the displacement of people in the region. Moreover, these same organizations sent out the early-warning message that the situation on the ground was deteriorating. In October and early November 1996, the fighting spread between the rebels commanded by Laurent Kabila, with support by the Rwandan Tutsi-dominated government and Rwandan-speaking Banyamulenge in Zaire, and the shrinking components of the Mobutu Sese Seko regime and the deposed Hutu (Interahamwe) militia. These developments seriously compromised the supply distribution operations run by humanitarian relief agencies. Indeed, with the attack on the Hutu militia-dominated refugee camps around Goma, just inside the Zaire border, the international agencies were compelled to cease operations.

Misplacing the Niche

GEOGRAPHICAL MISPLACEMENT

For all of its good will, and significant domestic reasons to be involved, Canada found it difficult to carry out the Zaire/Great Lakes operation. To begin with, the geographical placement (or misplacement) of the operation must be examined more closely. On the subject of Canada's relationship with the country and the people of the central African region, some evidence exists to justify the claim of a wide connection. Individual Canadians have devoted considerable time and effort building up expertise in Rwanda and Burundi in particular. Going back several decades, a number of Canadians have served in those countries, whether as missionaries (in the tradition of Father Georges-Henri Lévesque, who, among other activities, started the University of Rwanda) and/or educational volunteers (a notable example being Robert Fowler, Canada's Ambassador to the United Nations). A number of prominent Canadian diplomats earned solid experience in the subregion, not the least of whom was Raymond Chrétien, who served as Canada's ambassador to Zaire, Rwanda, and Burundi from 1978 to 1981.

Overlaying this relationship were a number of other features which provided Canada with at least some elements of a comparative advantage in forging a closer connection. One of these features was Canada's outward expression as a bilingual/bicultural country with a long-standing interest (and some generosity of spirit) in francophone Africa. Another was that this relationship came without many historical problems attached to it. Picking up on this theme of a natural fit between Canada and the area early on in the crisis, Ambassador Fowler declared: "Canada has spent a generation paying a lot of attention to development in the Great Lakes region [of Central Africa], principally in Rwanda and Burundi ... two little countries lost in the heart of darkness. [Canadians have] . . . no colonial baggage, no exploitation, and the ability to work in both languages."[5]

All of this involvement, however, was not enough to make Canada a legitimate candidate for alternative forms of leadership in the area. For all of Canada's people-to-people and cultural connections, the ambitious pursuit of a distinctive Canadian niche in central Africa in terms of humanitarian intervention may be judged to be a problematic fit. Contradicting the image of expansion, Canada in the 1990s looked like a country contracting its links with that part of the world. The most obvious sign of this trend was the geographic reorientation of the official development-assistance budget away from sub-Saharan Africa towards other geographic areas.[6]

This structural deficiency was compounded by a number of other situational factors that cut into Canada's credibility as a putative leader in a central African initiative. One key problem stemmed from Canada's own limited experience with peacekeeping/humanitarian intervention in the subregion. If, for example, J.L. Granatstein is correct in stating that an earlier generation of Canadian peacekeepers developed their expertise from their experience as "soldiers trained to fight the Russians in central Europe,"[7] the question must be asked whether these skills were readily transferable to the geography and conditions of central Africa. It is revealing, in this context, to note the failures not only of the 1994 UN Rwanda peacekeeping force (led by a Canadian general, Major-General Roméo Dallaire) but of the Congo peacekeeping force over three decades earlier. It is also sobering to reflect on the revelations concerning ethical/cultural deficiencies found in the Canadian participation in the Somalian mission in 1993.

FUNCTIONAL MISPLACEMENT

The other requisite for leadership that must be closely examined in the context of the Zaire/Great Lakes initiative centres on the need for a good store of resources. Possession of a surplus of will power must be complemented not only by acceptance as a legitimate geographical actor but also by adequate capabilities. In going out ahead of other countries, Canada ventured away from its traditional role as follower. In doing so, it provided some potential alternative sources of initiative and innovation in international politics. Yet, the obstacles in the way of Canada substituting for the more traditional—and structurally defined—modes of leadership remained imposing. To make the initiative work required more than just intangible resources, such as Canadian diplomatic skills. The venture also required a formidable array of tangible resources, especially military-related assets.

In the bid to get the initiative off the ground, Canadian state officials displayed a high degree of robustness in their diplomatic discourse/action. Prime Minister Chrétien's explanation for why the Canadian initiative was being launched centred on the absence of moral authority and an "out-in-front" style at the top end of the international system: "I was frustrated by the excuses ... Every hour of delay means more lost lives ... We have a moral duty to intervene before it is too late."[8]

As suggested above, the initiative appeared to mesh with many of Canadian strengths as an international actor. In the initial phase of the endeavour, Canada's ability to utilize international institutions generally, and the Security Council specifically, as the locus of inter-governmental negotiations came to the fore. In doing so, Canada demonstrated that it retained a marked capacity to play the multi-lateral diplomatic game. This type of diplomacy involved an enormous concentration of effort on a single issue by the entire cohort of senior foreign-policy makers. Much of the time and energy of Gordon Smith (deputy minister of Foreign Affairs), Paul Heinbecker (assistant deputy minister), James Bartleman (the prime minister's senior foreign policy/security adviser), and Robert Fowler (at the United Nations) was spent mobilizing support for Security Council resolution 1080 mandating the operation. Although impressive in its immediate payoff, this concentration of effort was hard to maintain beyond the initial stage.

In terms of the physical commitment, the initiative appeared to play up the best features of the Canadian military while playing down its weaknesses. As originally conceptualized by Canada, the mission was supposed to have two tracks. One of these centred on the provision of support for those refugees located in eastern Zaire through the provision and distribution of food and humanitarian supplies. The other track centred on efforts to facilitate the return of those refugees to Rwanda. Although mandated under section 7 of the UN Charter, therefore, the scope of engagement was to be limited. The initiative was conceived as a humanitarian as opposed to a peace-enforcement mission. Canadian personnel were to be deployed only by agreement with the parties on the ground, predicated on the non-use of force except in self-defence. The style of the mission was to be facilitative, placing the emphasis on support for relief operations and helping the United Nations High Commissioner for Refugees (UNHCR) to establish the conditions necessary for the voluntary repatriation of refugees, not towards a direct interventionist role.

This limited pattern of engagement underscored that the Canadian willingness to get involved at the state level was not open-ended. Equally, this approach reflected in a new and explicit fashion the constraint of the commitment-capability gap in Canadian international activities.[9] On the one hand, this problem relates to the question of overstretch of Canadian military personnel. Prime Minister Chrétien, in his initial press conference, played down the number of troops needed; both by talking about a maximum of 1500 military personnel and by adding that even this total might be an exaggeration in that it may be "quite possible that it will be less than that."[10] However, this type of estimate could be seriously questioned from a number of angles. With Canada's other commitments around the world (especially in Bosnia and Haiti, where Canada had in place 1000 and 700 peacekeepers respectively), one set of questions related to whether Canada could muster enough trained troops to meet this maximum level. The other set of questions focused on the issue of whether or not this maximum figure was too low of a calculation. Indeed, the belief that the number put forward by the prime minister might represent a minimum rather than a maximum took hold in the public debate as the calculation about the overall troop level of the multinational force rose from 10,000 to 20,000.

On the other hand, the problem of commitment-capability gap relates to a wide set of issues on the equipment needed to implement the mission effectively. Any humanitarian intervention required an enormous array of tools. Yet these resources needed to be mustered precisely at the time when the Canadian military was being subjected to a series of deep cuts. In the period 1991–2 to 1995–6, the Canadian defence budget was slashed from $12.83 billion to $10.5 billion.[11] As witnessed by the establishment of the highly mobile (but lightly armed) Disaster Assistance Response Team (DART), the Canadian military had extended its capacity in some specialized areas of high value to humanitarian operations. The difficulty, as highlighted by a wide number of observers, was that the cutbacks magnified "Canada's lack of truly multi-purpose, combat-capable military resources." By default as much as by design, the capabilities of the Canadian military in the Zaire/Great Lakes episode, as in a variety of other cases, was restricted to what may be called "quasi-military and non-military roles."[12]

The conditioning effect of this commitment-capability gap was visible throughout the Zaire/Great Lakes initiative. Although originally viewed as an opportunity to put a "coalition of the willing" together through diplomatic skill, the implementation process of the initiative revealed the enormous weight of US influence on Canadian international activity. While reflective of an autonomous sense of problem-identification and motivation, this initiative from below could not be put into action without the direct approval of the United States and a strong reliance on its massive technological/logistical base. Canada could signal that an initiative was necessary, and that such a mission fit in with its own definition of niche activity. But to activate a successful operation, US support was essential.

This weight of influence was imposed incrementally. Initially, Canada did have some considerable space in which to operate. On the diplomatic/institutional side, Canadian officials were placed in the position of managing the steering board which was to report back to the Security Council. On the military side, General Maurice Baril, in his capacity as commander-in-chief of the operation, chaired the meeting of military planners.

Throughout the initiative, however, Canadian state officials remained aware of the parameters imposed on this autonomous space for action. In declaratory terms, the US's capacity to make or break the initiative was publicly acknowledged. Prime Minister Chrétien allowed from the start that "the United States is vital to the success of any mission."[13] Subsequently, Gordon Smith made the same point in a more explicit fashion: "The Americans ... have the capacity to decide whether there is going to be an operation in eastern Zaire or not."[14]

At the early stages of planning, the need to get (and keep) the United States on side was linked directly to Canada's own commitment-capability problem. In complete contrast to the Canadian deficiencies, the Americans had a surplus of core military assets. In quantitative terms, the tip of this surplus was barely visible. The United States's early offer to supply troops was relatively modest: up to one thousand ground troops within the crisis area and an additional two to three thousand troops in nearby countries such as Kenya and Uganda.[15] What differentiated the American and Canadian military resources, apart from sheer size, related to the qualitative roles they were capable of taking on (most notably, airlift support).

This impressive set of assets provided the United States with enormous leverage. Despite the public posture of going along with Canada's out-in-front position, behind the scenes the United States worked hard to control the shape and conditions of the initiative. Instead of being allowed to focus their attention on working out the details of the composition and shared responsibilities of a multilateral force, Canadian state officials had constantly to react to bilateral American pressure. On 13 November 1996, for example, General Baril cancelled other meetings to fly to Washington to attend a Canada-US consultation. At this meeting, Canada achieved a number of procedural successes. Notwithstanding American pressure for a more diffuse leadership structure (with three deputy commanders), under which Baril confirmed his position as commander-in-chief. Moreover, along the lines of the Bosnian model, the force would have broad UN Security Council authority, with a steering board and contact group of key states. The United States, nevertheless, imposed what amounted to a veto on the operation. From a procedural perspective, the most significant outcome of this meeting was the stipulation that US forces remained under American command. While agreeing to give General Baril overall responsibility for the direction and coordination of the force, as commander he would not be allowed to assign responsibilities to American units without approval in advance.

The major agent of constraint was the US military, which constantly expressed concern about the rules of engagement for the multilateral force. As the terms of reference were initially discussed, the US military was open to the possibility of activities centred on the servicing of Goma airport and the creation of a five-kilometre-long humanitarian corridor, together with the establishment of temporary feeding stations designed to funnel refugees back to Rwanda. It was reluctant, however, to get involved in the direct distribution of relief supplies to refugees, the protection of relief supplies, and/or actually securing the airport. And it was utterly opposed to any plan that involved separation of the militias from the refugees, disarming of the militias, intervention between belligerents, and forced entry or control of the refugee camps. On the timescale, the US military was adamant that any mission should be short and have a clear departure date. Whereas Canada was willing to extend the deadline for a withdrawal from any mission to six months, the US military drew the line at four months.

Faced with these signs of organizational resistance by its closest allies, Canada maintained its efforts to get an effective force into the field. Immediately after the 21-22 November meeting of military personnel (held at the US European command centre in Stuttgart, Germany), in which consensus was reached only to set up a headquarters in the crisis area, Canadian officials showed that they were prepared to raise the stakes with respect to the agenda of the initiative. This new plan of operation would sanction enhanced reconnaissance/information gathering, a heightened command-and-control infrastructure to support further deployment in eastern Zaire, humanitarian airdrops deeper into Zaire, and even the possibility of escorted food convoys to assist refugees trapped to the west of Lake Kivu. At a Great Lakes crisis briefing, held at the United Nations on 26 November 1996, all of the members of the coalition (including the 14 members of the steering group) were given 36 hours to hand in the precise numbers of the contributions they were prepared to make.

The key event that exposed Canada's lack of capabilities, and broke its will to carry on further with the initiative, ultimately did not take place in the sites of multilateral or bilateral negotiations in Europe or North America. Rather, the catalyst for disengagement came on the ground in central Africa, amidst all the reports of a significant turnaround in the refugee situation between 15 November and 18 November. Although details of this event remained extremely sketchy, both the media and policy makers soon adopted two points. One of these centred on the massive return of some 550,000 to 600,000 Hutu refugees from Zaire to Rwanda. The other point concerned the fact that this movement appeared to be part of a process of voluntary repatriation. Instead of moving farther west in the aftermath of the rebel attacks on the camps around Goma, a large segment of the refugee population appeared to be separating themselves from the militia and voluntarily turning around to cross the border.

This unanticipated change in circumstances cut away much of what impetus lingered for the Zaire/Great Lakes initiative. Moving from its ambivalent position, the United States withdrew its support for the extended Canadian plan of operation. Although still on side with the task of facilitating the delivery of humanitarian aid to the returning refugees, the American military used the opportunity to announce a drastic reduction in its contribution. In the words of the American secretary of defense: "We are modifying our plans based on this dramatic change."[16] The number of troops committed to the mission was cut from four thousand to eight hundred. None of these remaining troops would be allowed to participate in any operation inside Zaire as part of a multinational force.

In the face of this last formidable component of the capability-commitment gap, Canada's will to continue with the initiative was ground down. Without adequate resources of its own to understand an increasingly confusing situation on the ground, lacking British and American support, and facing a wavering interest by the mainstream media, the Canadian government shifted its focus by the end of November from refining the interventionist strategy to implementing an exit strategy. By 3 December, the decision had been made to withdraw Canadian troops and command and to declare the mission over. While apparently quite prepared to make a unilateral declaration to this effect if necessary, a 13 December meeting in New York of the steering board of the multinational force curtailed the need for unilateral Canadian action. Canada had little trouble obtaining a consensus recommending to the UN secretary general that the mandate established under Security Council resolution 1080 be terminated by 31 December 1996.

Conclusion

At least in terms of public consumption, the reaction of Canadian state officials took the line that the initiative had proved a major instrumental success. For instance, Paul Heinbecker stated: "We are quite satisfied we have achieved the largest part of our mission."[17] This positive spin emphasized not only the compassionate motivation behind the mission but its effective nature in getting a difficult job done. By its willingness to embrace a constructive form of "just in time" diplomacy, Canada had made a difference. More precisely, the Canadian-led intervention was interpreted as having acted as a catalyst for movement to break open the crisis. As Prime Minister Chrétien pronounced in one of his year-end interviews: "The fact is that we woke up the international community—we triggered the movement for those people. And it is the biggest movement of human beings with no violence, you know, probably forever."[18]

To declare a victory, however, is not the same as to enjoy a moment of triumph. Any image of success for the Zaire/Great Lakes initiative remained highly contested. Instead of being universally acclaimed as a case in which Canada had acted in a timely and effective fashion, the mission was denounced by one strain of critics for having left large groups of Hutu refugees. These refugees faced retaliation and slaughter as the Kabila/Tutsi offensive, obscured from view in the forests in eastern Zaire, continued unabated. Even as the Canadian-led mission was wrapping up, a wide number of NGOs were calling for a renewal of a cross-border interventionist effort to save lives.[19]

Another strain of criticism took a more restrictionist line. From one perspective, this criticism was based on a narrower view of the national interest, with a distrust for any form of activity not directly concerned with the immediate safety of Canada (and Canadians) from outside threats. From another perspective, the criticism was more pragmatic in nature, based on a fear of Canada being drawn more deeply into a mission in the central African region without a full appreciation of all the complexity, uncertainty, and risks attached to this targeted activity. The point made explicit was that the Zaire/Great Lakes initiative lay outside Canada's zone of influence, interest, and comfort level.[20]

The only commonality, among these very divergent criticisms, is the view that the Zaire/Great Lakes case was a problematic case for Canada to go out in front of an international mission. Rather than being portrayed as a decisive player, in moving from the position of follower to a leader on an issue-specific basis, Canada was perceived as still constrained by the structure and disciplines of the international system. If Canada was credited with the display of a good deal of will power and commitment, its lack of the "right" sort of capabilities was also underscored. Instead of being a prime example of an episode in which Canada's effective store of "soft power" could be brought to bear to address an international problem,[21] the Zaire/Great Lakes initiative highlighted the ingrained significance of the military component of the security agenda. While the Canadian strengths, centred on entrepreneurial and technical forms of leadership, could be appreciated (and prove useful), these same strengths could be quickly sapped if, and when, placed in situations where military capabilities became vital.

NOTES

Funding for this chapter has been provided by the Social Sciences and Humanities Research Council, as part of a wider project on "Diplomatic Puzzles: Canadian Issue-Specific Activity in Comparative Perspective." The comments provided by the other participants in the February 1998 workshop are warmly appreciated.

1   On this logic see Andrew F. Cooper, "In Search of Niches: Saying 'Yes' and Saying 'No' in Canada's International Relations," *Canadian Foreign Policy* 3/3 (winter 1995), 113; Evan H. Potter, "Niche Diplomacy as Canadian Foreign Policy," *International Journal* LII (winter 1996-7), 25-38.

2   As related in one journalistic account, Raymond Chrétien urged the prime minister to "play and play fast." David Pugliese, "Nobel Fever," *Saturday Night* (May 1997). See also John Kirton, "Foreign Policy Under the Liberals: Prime Ministerial Leadership in the Chrétien Government's Foreign Policy-making Process," in Fen Osler Hampson, Maureen Appel Molot, and Martin Rudner, eds., *Canada among Nations 1997: Asia Pacific Faceoff* (Ottawa, 1997).

3   Transcript, press conference, Prime Minister Jean Chrétien, CBC Newsworld, 16:00, 12 November 1996.

4   On the Quebec dimension see Hugh Winsor, "Rescue mission a proud endeavour," *Globe and Mail*, 15 November 1996; Terrance Willis, "PM keeps one eye on Quebec when developing Zaire plan," Montreal *Gazette*, 19 November 1996. For a flavour of the positive reception the initiative received initially in Quebec, see Jocelyn Coulon, "Un grand moment pour la diplomatie canadienne," *Le Devoir*, 15 November 1996.

5   Quoted in Hugh Winsor, "Envoy takes on toughest task," *Globe and Mail*, 1 November 1996.

6 Jeff Sallot, "The changing face of foreign aid," *Globe and Mail*, 13 February 1993. See also David R. Black and Jean-Philippe Thérien with Andrew Clark, "Moving with the Crowd: Canadian Aid to Africa," *International Journal*, 51 (spring 1996), 264-7.

7 Testimony to the special joint committee of the Senate and of the House of Commons on Canada's defence policy, Minutes of Proceedings and Evidence, 19 April 1994, 2:10.

8 Quoted in Jeff Sallott and Paul Knox, "Canada pushes U.S. for support," *Globe and Mail*, 13 November 1996.

9 For a recent appraisal see Louis Nastro and Kim Richard Nossal, "The Commitment-Capability Gap: Implications for Canadian Foreign Policy in the Post-Cold War Era," *Canadian Defence Quarterly* (autumn 1997), 19-22.

10 Transcript, press conference, Prime Minister Jean Chrétien, CBC Newsworld, 16:00, 12 November 1996.

11 Canada, Department of National Defence, *1994 Defence White Paper* (Ottawa: Ministry of Supply and Services Canada, 1994). On these cuts, see Claire Turenne Sjolander, "Cashing in on the 'Peace Dividend': National Defence in the Post-Cold War World," in Gene Swimmer, ed., *How Ottawa Spends 1996-97: Life under the Knife* (Ottawa: Carleton University Press, 1996), 253-82.

12 Nastro and Nossal, "The Commitment-Capability Gap," 19.

13 Quoted in Barbara Crossette, "Canada proses Zaire aid force," New York *Times*, 13 November 1996.

14 Quoted in Hugh Winsor, "Mission to Africa hung up on confusion over need," *Globe and Mail*, 23 November 1996.

15 James Bennet, "Size of U.S. force bound for Africa is cut below 1,000," New York *Times*, 20 November 1996.

16 United States, Department of Defense, DOD News Briefing, Secretary of Defense William J. Perry, "Comments on Zaire," 19 November 1996.

17 Quoted in Stephen Handelman, "Canada to halt African mission," Toronto *Star*, 14 December 1996.

18 Global TV interview, quoted in David Pugliese, "Nobel Fever," *Saturday Night*, May 1997, 62; Allan Thompson, "African rescue

mission receives scathing reviews," Toronto *Star*, 22 December 1996.

19 The CBC's Fifth Estate documentary on the mission, aired on 18 November 1997, developed more fully this theme of under-commitment.

20 One representative illustration of this restrictionist view is provided by Peter Worthington in his article "What are we doing in Africa?" Toronto *Sun*, 19 November 1996.

21 See, for example, Lloyd Axworthy, "Canadian Foreign Policy in a Changing World," speech to the National Forum on Foreign Policy, Winnipeg, 13 December 1996, *Canadian Speeches* (January/February 1997), 19.

Chapter Seven

Canada and Helms-Burton: The Perils of Coalition Building

Evan H. Potter

Introduction

On 24 February 1996 Cuba shot down two unarmed civilian planes flown by anti-Castro dissidents from Miami. Under intense pressure from Cuban-Americans, United States President Bill Clinton signed the Cuban Liberty and Democratic Solidarity (Libertad) Act, known as the Helms-Burton Act, into law on 12 March. This marked the beginning of a shrill diplomatic war between the United States and some of its closest allies, a war over the right of one nation to decide the trading partners of other nations.

Some of the United States's closest allies, such as Canada, the European Union (EU), and Mexico, found the American policy of further entrenching the existing 35-year-old US embargo against Cuba and the encouragement of foreign divestment from the island to be both contrary to the spirit of a liberal international trading order and absolutely the worst way of bringing down the Castro dictatorship. A loose, very public alliance against Helms-Burton was thus developed around these two positions. Canada, with both a historical track record of opposition to the American embargo and significant commercial exposure on the island, took a particular interest in playing a leadership role in this coalition.

This chapter examines the forces at play when Canada, Mexico, and the EU attempted to forge a loose coalition in 1996-7 to counteract the Helms-Burton Act. How did the particular nature of the United States's bilateral relations with the individual members of this coalition affect the success or failure of the extraterritorial application of this US law? The essay's major argument is that, while Canada may be a natural coalition leader, it faced particular difficulty building a coalition of like-minded states on a foreign policy issue that was driven by powerful American domestic interests.

Canada has taken an autonomous approach to Cuba since 1959,[1] never severing relations as the United States did. In 1979 Canada cut off bilateral aid to Cuba because of Havana's involvement in the war in Angola, but aid was reinstated in 1994 through non-governmental agencies. Canada has always maintained full diplomatic representation with Cuba. Total trade between Canada and Cuba—while never significant when compared to Canada's other trading relations—nevertheless doubled between 1992 and 1997 to $600 million. At the same time, despite American claims to the opposite, Ottawa repeatedly raised its human-rights concerns at the most senior levels in Cuba. Canada also co-sponsored resolutions on human-rights abuses in Cuba at the United Nations Commission on Human Rights in Geneva.

The Canadian reaction to Helms-Burton was swift but, as will be shown, largely symbolic. Antidote legislation was passed unanimously by the Canadian Parliament in record time. The legislation allows companies found liable under the act to counter-sue and win judgments in Canadian courts that would offset any penalties imposed in the United States; it authorizes "blocking orders" to prevent enforcement of US judgments in Canada; and it allows the federal government to impose fines of up to C$1.5 million against Canadian companies, and up to C$150,000 against individuals, for complying with the act. On the international front, in June 1996 Canada pushed forward a unanimous resolution at the Organization of American States (OAS) to have the Inter-American Judicial Committee assess the legality of the act. The committee later ruled that Helms-Burton did not conform to international law. Ottawa also argued that the act was a violation of the North American Free Trade Aggreement since it would make Canadian investment in the United States subject to less favourable treatment.

Having accused the previous Conservative government of being a "camp follower of the United States," the Liberal government found in Helms-Burton a convenient rallying point for the "independent

foreign policy" that it had called for while in opposition. The Chrétien government was at this time also smarting from the public criticism of its "trade-before-human-rights" approach to China. Cuba
became one of the few valuable symbols in Ottawa's foreign policy.
With polls showing that 71 per cent of Canadians were soundly behind the government in its denunciation of the US legislation, the
Canadian prime minister and his trade and foreign-affairs ministers
were all extraordinarily vocal on Canada's Cuba policy. In an unusu-
al display of partnership with the federal government, a coalition of
Canadian non-governmental organizations (NGOs) led by Oxfam
Canada, and including unions and national farmers' groups, went so
far as to launch a boycott-Florida campaign. As one senior Canadian
official commented, Canada's unified reaction to Helms-Burton was
entirely predictable, "like mother's milk," in that it showed that
Canada was independent from the United States.

In late January 1997, Foreign Affairs Minister Lloyd Axworthy and
Secretary of State Christine Stewart made a 24-hour visit to Cuba to
sign a 14-point declaration on human rights. Initiatives included
judicial training, academic exchanges, and the formation of a Citizens' Complaints Commission within the Cuban National Assembly.
For Axworthy, the trip signified Canada's long-standing policy of engagement with the Castro regime, the belief being that it was better
to "work from inside and talk across the table instead of pillorying
[Castro] from a megaphone in a Capital Hill committee room."[2] It
also reflected his attempt to position Canada's foreign policy through
"effective influence."

Although the declaration in Canadian eyes was unprecedented
because it committed the Cubans, for the first time, to work publicly
with Canada on human-rights and governance issues, it cut little ice
with the Americans. Nor did subsequent seminars organized by
Canada on children's rights (in Havana) and on women's rights (in
Ottawa). Canada was careful in its public announcements not to link
the Axworthy/Stewart visit to its rejection of Helms-Burton, but the
visit was nonetheless criticized by both the American administration
("collaboration with a dictator," said the State Department's
spokesperson; "sincere but misguided," said President Clinton) and
Congress ("another finger in the eye of the US," said a spokesperson

for Senator Jesse Helms). Clinton's special envoy on Cuba, Stuart Eizenstat, was equally dismissive, suggesting that the Complaints Commission was a far cry from an independent ombudsman and would probably end up dealing with electrical outages rather than human-rights abuses. Given the Canadians' apparent leverage with Havana, the Clinton administration wondered aloud why Ottawa did not insist on reforms to the Cuban penal code to eliminate political crimes, the establishment of independent NGOs, and the establishment of a free press.

The war of words continued. Canadian officials countered that the United States was suffering a case of "selective indignation" given its refusal to impose equally harsh sanctions on another human-rights-abusing regime—China. The Americans would often respond that they did not need any lessons on such indignation from a country that was intent on mobilizing the international community to punish Nigeria's generals through economic sanctions. The US reaction to another whirlwind visit to Cuba by Prime Minister Chrétien in the spring of 1998 was more muted but also one of anger at what it considered unnecessary provocation (a "propaganda bonanza" for Castro) by its northern neighbour. In contrast, Pope John Paul II's visit to Cuba a few months prior to the Chrétien visit was seen in a much more positive light by the US administration. There is, of course, a delicious irony to this diplomatic contretemps: had the Canadians succeeded in getting what the Americans would have considered more meaningful reforms out of the Cubans, they would have undermined the entire US strategy of using isolation to create democracy on the island. Canada's "failure" to secure major reforms was in fact the best outcome for the United States.

On the surface, then, it would appear that Canada—having self-consciously decided that it would be, in the words of Foreign Minister Axworthy, an "active Western Hemisphere player"—was in a relatively strong position, morally and legally, to lead an international coalition against Helms-Burton. The answers to why this leadership was weak and why there did not appear to be full commitment by the coalition's members lay in the complex bilateral relationships between these countries and the United States.

The Impact of Helms-Burton on Canada-US Relations: Tempest in a Teapot

Judging from the extensive media coverage, one could be forgiven for thinking that Helms-Burton had caused irreparable fissures in some of the United States's most important bilateral relations. But the act's impact should be put into perspective. Although the United States probably did not anticipate such a visceral reaction from its allies, the act did not alter the overall "tones" of US relations with Canada, the EU, and Mexico.

The Clinton administration understood as much. So did Ottawa, it just did not say so publicly. As Eizenstat quipped at a conference on Helms-Burton in 1997, the reaction to the act had been a "tea party" when compared to other bilateral matters. To illustrate the point, he claimed that Canada could have gone to the United Nations to attack American actions but chose not to. With the Pacific coast salmon dispute looming and ongoing problems with softwood lumber (worth $3 billion alone), the Canada-Cuba trading relationship was hardly worth drawing a line in the sand over. Indeed, despite the fact that the United States upped the diplomatic ante when it barred four executives from a Canadian company doing business in Cuba from entering the United States in March 1997, and despite Wal-Mart stores in Canada being forced to remove Cuban-made pajamas from their shelves, Ottawa was still unwilling to challenge its neighbour in the courts. Some in Ottawa considered a tit-for-tat strategy in which Canada would have started to harass and ban US executives travelling to Canada; however, this would have involved a potential amendment to Canada's Immigration Act and such a notion was soon dropped.

Had it chosen to act, Ottawa certainly had recourse to some powerful, although somewhat untested, judicial procedures to challenge the validity of Helms-Burton. The act violated the spirit and letter of NAFTA, for it made Canadian investment in the United States subject to less favourable treatment by virtue of the fact that Canadian firms' assets there would be liable. It also violated NAFTA's expropriation clause. Third, countries such as Canada were facing a growing number of secondary boycotts as a result of a plethora of American federal, state, and municipal sanctions. For this reason all the steps were put in place for a NAFTA challenge. But why did action actually stop short of demanding a panel?

The procedural and technical reasons for not taking further action offer a useful camouflage for the more substantive political reasons. For instance, the procedural requirements for a NAFTA dispute-resolution panel were not in place and, had the Canadians suggested panel members and the Americans refused, there would have been no panel. This would surely have been embarrassing to Ottawa. Arthur Eggleton, then international-trade minister, and his advisers felt that because the NAFTA panel was not as far advanced procedurally as its World Trade Organization (WTO) counterpart, calling for such a panel could undermine the credibility of NAFTA as a whole, especially if the Americans were pushed to invoke a national-security exemption.[3] Fundamentally, Canada did not wish to forsake the overall tone of its bilateral relations with the United States for one piece of extraterritorial legislation. But these technical reasons would clearly not fly politically as a justification for pulling back. President Clinton, by agreeing to suspend terms of the act that allowed for prosecution of Canadian companies, gave Ottawa just the "out" that it needed, allowing it both to bluster *and* not to pursue a more vigorous strategy that would have seen certain provisions of NAFTA litigated in international law.

Eizenstat was right. The Helms-Burton Act had not sent Canada-United States relations off the rails. Unlike Canadian gunboat diplomacy over the Spanish fishing vessel *Estai* in 1995, which was to have negative repercussions for Canada-EU relations, the Canadian stance on Cuba was long-standing and well understood by Canada-watchers in Washington. The acerbic rhetoric on both sides was designed largely for domestic audiences. The Canadian government's lack of desire to push the United States too far, the Europeans' negative reaction to Canada's reluctance to pursue the United States under NAFTA, Mexico's own unique history of bilateral relations with the United States as well as its discomfort with some of the "democratic engagement" language surrounding the issue—all pointed to the difficulty of achieving anything more than a loose coalition against Helms-Burton. And Canada faced a further dilemma. On the one hand, its ability to lead a concerted coalition of like-minded states to fight Helms-Burton would solidify its reputation as a "player" in the hemisphere, where the Americans were already complaining that they were "tripping over" Canadians; on the other, Helms-Burton was such a volatile American political issue that it had the potential, if Ottawa chose to pursue it aggressively, of doing long-term damage to Canada-United States relations.

Europe and Mexico: Also Reluctant Partners

In response to the extraterritorial US legislation in 1996, Canada, the EU, and Mexico all enacted broader blocking statutes, which barred compliance with and neutralized the effects of the US secondary boycott. They seemed destined to be natural allies in forcing if not a repeal of the act itself then at least concessions in managing it.

There was general agreement among the three countries on three points. First of all, the act was a political/bilateral United States-Cuba issue rather than a legal problem. Second, the United States would never accept such extraterritorial application from another country. Third, while the act might have negligible impact on world trade, the impact of the legislation for the international system was far greater in light of what it signalled about growing US unilateralism and willingness to use secondary-boycott legislation that defies the principles of a rules-based international trading system. The Europeans were particularly concerned about the precedent that would be set if the United States were to invoke national security "so lightly" in a WTO dispute-settlement panel. Hugo Paeman, the EU ambassador to the United States in 1997, went so far as to state that it would be like "injecting a virus into the international economic system that could grow as other nations take reprisals of their own."[4]

The Europeans wasted no time in reacting. In May 1996 the European Parliament resolved to condemn the US legislation. By the end of that year, the EU had requested and implemented a WTO settlement panel, adopted national legislation to block the act, changed procedures governing the entry of US firms to Europe, and prepared a list of US companies that had filed for compensation.

As in the Canadian case, the Europeans had no desire to antagonize overtly the Americans and create the potential for an outbreak of nasty trade conflict similar to the "chicken war" of the 1960s, which had spilled over into the political domain. The Helms-Burton Act came at a time when the post-Cold War transatlantic architecture was being reconfigured and neither the Americans nor the Europeans had a desire to let this process unravel over Cuba. Like the Canadian strategy, the EU approach was not to attack the whole act but to target the secondary-embargo provision and extraterritorial aspects (for example, denial of transit and prohibition of loans to EU firms). In addition, the EU completed a cooperation agreement with Cuba in January 1997 in which the Cubans reluctantly accepted conditions tying aid to political reform. This actually went farther than any Canadian agreement with Havana in linking economic assistance to reform. Washington's spin was that the EU had seen the light and was gradually shifting its position. In fact, as the Europeans reminded the Americans, such conditions are a standard feature of all the EU's cooperation agreements; Cuba had not been singled out for special treatment.

The Europeans were not at all happy with Canada's reluctance to call for the NAFTA panel. They also felt that Canada was trying to ride their coat-tails by agreeing to be only an observer at the WTO panel. Ottawa's official response was that, if it had acted as a full member of the WTO panel, it would have eliminated its ability to make a NAFTA challenge.

Following high-level brinksmanship over Helms-Burton in early 1997, the United States and the EU signed an agreement in April on the principles governing the extraterritorial application of law and suspending the WTO panel until a later date. Over the course of the spring Ottawa had grown progressively more suspicious of European motives. The commission was pushing Ottawa to launch a NAFTA challenge while all along engaging in bilateral negotiations with the Americans. The Europeans, after having supported Canada's hard-line stance in 1996, refused to "trilateralize" their agreement with the Americans to include Canada because of their continuing pique at Ottawa's reluctance to proceed with the NAFTA panel. Or so they said. It was more likely that they realized they could get a quicker deal with two sets of negotiators rather than with three. The Americans were meanwhile giving Ottawa regular updates on the state of their negotiations with the Europeans. Continuing to hang like a pall over Canada's relations with Europe was the "turbot war," which, in the eyes of the Europeans, significantly undercut Canada's credibility as a champion of international law. It appears that neither the Europeans nor the Canadians were entirely forthright about their true intentions, making it difficult to maintain a coalition.

In many ways the Mexican dimension of the story is much less opaque. With the signing of the NAFTA in 1993, Canada and Mexico saw each other as natural allies in any attempt to blunt the edge of American power in the hemisphere. Helms-Burton offered just such an opportunity, which was made all the more attractive by European support.

The highest degree of Canadian-Mexican cooperation to combat Helms-Burton occurred at the initial stages and peaked in 1996 with Canada's Foreign Extra-Territorial Measures Act. Following the example set by Canada, Mexico enacted its own clawback legislation. Canada took the lead in preparing for a NAFTA panel, with Mexico providing support. At this point Ottawa and Mexico City presented a united front.

However, Ottawa could not count on Mexico City's subsequent support. With its own problems in Chiapas, Mexico had no interest in the human-rights dimensions of the conflict, while Canada clearly did. For Mexico, the concern with Helms-Burton was exclusively about the extraterritorial application of US law. Mexico also had fewer commercial interests in Cuba than did Canada. But perhaps the most important reason why Mexico could offer only limp support was the sudden and worsening turn in its own bilateral relations with the United States. Since the time of the peso devaluation in 1994, Mexico had to contend with a US Congress that would not authorize a multibillion dollar emergency bailout and with regular threats by Washington to decertify it (with loss of US assistance for anti-drug activity) in the war on drugs.

As was the case with the Canadian and European policy makers, there did not appear to be a great enthusiasm among Mexican policy makers to adopt an offensive strategy against the act since this would have further exacerbated existing bilateral tensions with the United States. Mexico lined up behind Canada, but if Ottawa was not going to take the plunge, neither was Mexico City.

Conclusion

Canadian policy makers came to the conclusion that, although a NAFTA or WTO challenge could have turned into a moral victory for the EU, Canada, and Mexico, it would not have changed US domestic law. They worried that the processes would "lose steam within a year," with little in the way of accrued results for their efforts; Helms-Burton was a domestic political issue for Washington, not one of international trade. For this reason Ottawa favoured the harassment tactic. "Keep the issue alive so long as we are not provoked to take action," remarked one senior official.[5] As long as no more companies were named under the act,[6] Canada could blithely pursue a strategy of harassment that played well domestically but did not incur any real costs. Following this logic, Ottawa's strategy—despite pressure from the Europeans and with the Mexicans taking their cues from the Canadians—was to maintain the threat rather than carry it out. The value of this tactic was bolstered by its open-endedness. That is to say, it did not preclude Ottawa from eventually pursuing the WTO and NAFTA tracks. Nor did the tactic constrain Canadian officials from further "multilateralizing" the dispute through the Multilateral Agreement on Investment. The US legislation was but the tip of a plethora of unilateral sanctions and secondary boycotts being deployed by the Americans.

More generally, the Helms-Burton episode illustrates the nature of coalition building against the United States. Above all, it highlights Canada's ambiguity about where exactly it wanted to be located on the issue: out in front as an issue-specific leader (as it saw itself on the Nigeria and land mines initiatives), or more narrowly tending to its bilateral relationship with Washington. Although the extraterritorial implications of Helms-Burton were clearly important to those opposing Washington's position, it was not so important as to imperil the bilateral relationships of the loose coalition.

NOTES

An earlier version of this chapter was presented as a paper at the annual meeting of the Canadian Political Science Association, Memorial University, 10 June 1997. A second version was published as a paper for the Centre for International Relations at Queen's University, Kingston, Ontario.

1   For a history of Canada-Cuba relations, see John M. Kirk, "In Search of a Canadian Foreign Policy Towards Cuba," *Canadian Foreign Policy* 2/2 (fall 1994), 73-84; John M. Kirk, Peter McKenna, and Julia Sagebien, "Back in Business: Canada-Cuba Relations after 50 Years," *The Focal Papers* (March 1995), 5-28.

2   As quoted in "Canada plans to groom relations with Cuba, foreign minister says," Minnoapolis *Star Tribune*, 14 February 1997, 8. On the transition from a more diffuse Canadian foreign policy to one that is more selective and effective, see Evan H. Potter, "Niche Diplomacy as Canadian Foreign Policy," *International Journal* 52/1 (winter 1996-7), 25-38.

3   See the discussion by Peter McKenna on the role of the US Branch in directing the position of the Department of Foreign Affairs and International Trade. Peter McKenna, "Canada and Helms-Burton: Up Close and Personal," *Canadian Foreign Policy* 4/3, 1997, 7–20.

4   From a conference sponsored by the Center for International Policy, "Helms-Burton: A Loose Cannon?" Washington, D.C., 9-11 February 1998.

5   Senior official, Department of Foreign Affairs and International Trade, telephone interview, Ottawa, 5 June 1997.

6   However, unlike Title III, Title IV is not discretionary, which means that if it comes to the attention of Congress the Canadian companies must be pursued.

Chapter Eight

Mission Diplomacy or Arctic Haze? Canada and Circumpolar Cooperation

Peter J. Stoett

Introduction

Seen from a distance, the creation of the Arctic Council in 1996 appeared a progressive step. Not only will it involve northern peoples in its affairs—they have been granted the rather awkward status of "permanent participants"—but it has a mandate to deal with issues related to sustainable development. It will consist of eight Arctic states: Canada, Denmark (Greenland), Finland, Iceland, Norway, Russia, Sweden, and the United States. As we become increasingly aware of the environmental problems affecting the Arctic region, this multilateral body seems vital.[1] It provides a unique forum "in which all legitimate stakeholders can debate Arctic issues, and weave a burgeoning collection of issue-specific initiatives into a coherent whole."[2]

However, the Arctic Council may be generating significant Arctic haze as well. Is it really necessary? Will it force governments to put more resources into the preservation of the north? Or will it simply facilitate excessive industrial development, particularly in the resource-extraction sector, and co-opt indigenous voices in the process? While the appointment of Mary Simon as circumpolar ambassador for Ottawa may be viewed as a symbolic victory for the Inuit, it could also be seen in a less flattering light: one anonymous respondent to a survey undertaken for this chapter suggested that the appointment "effectively muzzled an effective government critic." Further, the council was able to acquire American participation only after agreeing that military matters were not going to be discussed. Since military operations have resulted in much of the pollution still faced by northern natives, does this limitation render the council inconsequential?

From a Canadian foreign-policy perspective, the Arctic would seem a reasonable—indeed, quintessential—source of inspiration for what Andrew Cooper and Evan Potter refer to as niche diplomacy.[3] It is plainly in Canada's interests to pursue mutually advantageous arrangements in an area so integral to the Canadian state; and, since there are obvious human rights and environmental concerns to be addressed, the council moves towards diplomatic "operationalization" of the most recent Ottawanian buzzphrase, *human security.*

However, the perspective that emerges here is less than celebratory. Not only is there surprisingly widespread dissatisfaction with the council's present condition (it seems mired in bureaucratic mud); but the idea that Canada is playing a true leadership role is refuted by many engaged in the fields of Arctic research. Too often, multilateral diplomatic activity for its own sake fails to alter significantly the situation on the ground. One could even suggest that it detracts from the tougher job of actually doing something.

There have been many bilateral initiatives on polar affairs, involving the same states that have composed the Arctic Council and dating back to US-Russian scientific cooperation in 1879. Multilateral cooperation has been harder to come by, though there have been some notable exceptions. The 1911 Treaty for the Preservation and Protection of Fur Seals was one of the first marine mammal-protection regimes. Another important development for wildlife conservation was the 1973 International Agreement on the Conservation of Polar Bears, signed by Canada, Denmark, Norway, Russia, and the United States. A special provision in the text of the 1982 Law of the Sea allows coastal states to enforce pollution prevention against other states' ships; this right occurs within the 200-nautical mile Exclusive Economic Zone, where ice is present most of the year and where pollution could cause major harm to the environment, validating Canada's 1970 unilateral legislation.[4] The closest thing to the Arctic Council, however, is the Barents Euro-Arctic Council (Finland, Norway, Russia, Sweden) and a broader regional council which includes members of the European Union Commission, founded in 1993.

More directly relevant to the Arctic Council was the establishment of the Arctic Environmental Protection Strategy (AEPS) in 1991, which involved several international organizations. The AEPS incorporates five major programs:

1) AMAP—the Arctic Monitoring and Assessment Program, which researches chemical and radioactive contaminants, oil, heavy metals, noise, and acidification;
2) CAFF—the Program for the Conservation of Arctic Flora and Fauna, which assesses the condition of wildlife and biodiversity;
3) PAME—Protection of the Arctic Marine Environment, which examines the findings of AMAP and CAFF and recommends and promotes national and international legal regimes to address problems;
4) EPPR—Emergency Protection, Preparedness, and Response, which is supposed to plan for nuclear or gas-line (etc.) accidents; and
5) SDU—Sustainable Development and Utilization.[5]

In 1996 it became clear that the AEPS would be subsumed by the Arctic Council, and the SDU evolved into a task force/working group in that capacity. This increased the emphasis on long-term thinking and at least partly represented the wishes of indigenous groups concerned with both the excesses of oil and mining extraction, on the one hand, and the anti-fur and anti-whaling lobby, on the other.

The AEPS is the cornerstone of multilateral environmental diplomacy in the Arctic. Though there were complaints about its emphasis on monitoring and recommending as opposed to implementing corrective policies, it was firmly established and has produced various reports, such as the one mentioned above, that help guide us toward future needs. However, many feel that national governments did not put sufficient resources behind it and that it lacked political clout. Perhaps the formation of the Arctic Council will remedy this institutional lacuna. On the other hand, if it does not, then the old AEPS framework might be missed.

From a Canadian perspective, it is clear that the Arctic plays a large role in the national imagination. It is a wealthy resource base but also a source of artistic inspiration and, perhaps, identity. John Kirton writes that the Arctic can be viewed as an "emotional and geographic preserve."[6] A similar sentiment was evident during the recent hearings of the House of Commons Standing Committee on Foreign Affairs on "Canada and the Circumpolar World." With a large indigenous population in the north, and with questions of sovereignty over Arctic waters still on the agenda, generating increased multilateral activity on the Arctic would seem a natural goal, especially in the wake of the Cold War, which formerly prohibited any sustained interaction across East-West lines.

On the other hand, the remoteness of the region, its relative weightlessness in the electoral process, and the complexity of impending land-claims negotiations—over and above the establishment of a new territory, Nunavut—dampen federal enthusiasm for matters Arctic. There is more direct concern with Arctic matters that affect the south or with broader programs confronting non-Arctic regions such as global warming and ozone-layer thinning.[7] Since these questions are dealt with elsewhere (the UN Conference on Environment and Development, the UN Commission on Sustainable Development, the Kyoto Conference, the Montreal Protocol), we would be mistaken to assume that Ottawa will expend a great deal of energy on Arctic policy.

There is little doubt that Canada has played a vital role in the establishment of the Arctic Council, but we should avoid painting this as a story of unique Canadian leadership. Contextual factors are as relevant: it is quite clear that, without the end of the Cold War, there would be no council. Even so, military matters are out-of-bounds. Further, several important academic and diplomatic initiatives preceded recent gestures from Ottawa. The 1977 Berger report, which culminated in a revival of interest in Arctic resource issues, urged the establishment of a circumpolar program of research to determine the long-term impact of industrialization. A speech by Mikhail Gorbachev in Murmansk, on 1 October 1987, was instrumental in getting future Russian cooperation off the ground (Gorbachev stressed the need to cooperate in several areas, including science, environmental protection, marine transport, and denuclearization, though he excluded a key naval base in Murmansk). And Finland proposed that circumpolar cooperation be institutionalized in the mid-1980s; this gradually evolved into the "Rovaniemi Process" that, with significant input and pressure from indigenous groups, established the AEPS in January 1991.[8]

Fair is fair, however: Brian Mulroney did first formally articulate the idea for an Arctic council, in a speech at St Petersburg (then Leningrad) in November 1989. In 1990 the Walter and Duncan Gordon Charitable Foundation established a panel to promote the establishment of the council. In the early 1990s, what was then known as the Arctic Council Panel produced a "Draft Declaration on the Establishment of an Arctic Council," and the Department of External Affairs engaged in bilateral talks with the Scandinavian countries and the United States. The Inuit Circumpolar Conference (ICC) and Canada both pushed for the institutionalized inclusion of indigenous groups. The initial diplomatic difficulty resided not with the Scandinavians or even the Russians but with the Americans. That Canada was eventually able to get the Americans on board might be viewed as a victory, especially in light of the past dispute over sovereignty and the Northwest Passage.

A 1992 conference in Fairbanks on the "Changing Role of the US in the Circumpolar World" signified the beginning of a shift in American thinking; this was strengthened by a declaration in Nuuk in 1993 that the United States officially supported the idea of broadening the AEPS to deal with sustainable development as long-term issue. (At this time Canada agreed to take the lead in developing terms of reference and a plan to broaden the AEPS to deal with sustainable development.) This did not mean immediate support for the creation of the council, which the Americans felt would detract from funding priorities elsewhere and in essence duplicate ongoing circumpolar efforts. Once it became apparent that the other states were prepared to go ahead and create a non-US Council, however, the Clinton administration decided to join in, albeit with the firm stipulation that military matters were off limits.

This last point has raised great concern for several reasons. Within the North American disarmament movement there is some history of holding the Arctic up as a potential denuclearized zone, akin to the Antarctic. During the Cold War this was viewed as chimerical in Washington and Moscow; the Arctic was key geopolitical space. But in the post-Cold War era expectations rose that this goal might be reached. Secondly, the American military has left a mess in the Canadian Arctic and the terms of its clean-up have been dissatisfying to many Canadians. Though an agreement has been reached that gives Ottawa some compensation, it is a highly controversial one, requiring the purchase of American products and limited to a few of the Distant Early Warning line sites affected. Finally, indigenous people are inclined to display solidarity with those protesting low-level NATO training flights in northern Labrador, and the council may have been a means to put some pressure on both the Canadian and American governments.

However, it was unrealistic to expect the southern superpower to open what has been a secretive book to an institution with not only considerable growing pains but a multilateral context. Further, it is unclear whether or not the Russians really wanted serious military matters to be discussed, either; though it is obvious that any help Russia can acquire to clean up radioactivity is welcome, it is receiving some of this through bilateral agreements with various states and a trilateral agreement with the United States and Norway. So we might be somewhat circumspect when viewing the "frustration" Ottawa (the capital city of a NATO country) experienced on this matter. A ranking State Department official suggested that the real reason for American reluctance was related to a suspicion that the AEPS was adequate, given the resources cost-cutting governments could put into environmental protection in the Arctic. In other words, the United States was not willing to devote a significantly disproportionate level of funding to AEPS programs and did not see how creating a council would help. Nonetheless, there was enough support for the idea of the latter to see it through.

The Arctic Council, declared a celebratory press release, is a "high-level permanent intergovernmental forum to provide for co-operation, co-ordination and interaction among the Arctic states, the Arctic indigenous communities and other Arctic inhabitants on common Arctic issues [including] economic and social development, improved health conditions and cultural well-being."[9] It will be run on consensus, not a majority-voting system. Non-Arctic states, intergovernmental and inter-parliamentary organizations, and select non-governmental organizations (NGOs) will be observers and three indigenous organizations are given "permanent participant" status. However, it is clear that the council has little concrete political power, and that its agenda—though broader by definition than that of the AEPS—has limitations. Further, many complain that the Inuvik text is weakened by its emphasis on process as opposed to action (this, one might argue, is the inevitable result of a multilateral context), and that even when it comes to process the council secretariat has been dreadfully slow establishing firm foundations. Some researchers involved in Arctic affairs have expressed (in an anonymous capacity) the opinion that the AEPS was at least active and running and it was preferable to have that than what is slowly becoming perceived—prematurely, it is to be hoped—as the current institutional abyss. On the other hand, the availability of a central secretariat may be a lifesaver in the event of a large-scale environmental catastrophe.

There is some temptation to leap into analytic invention here and claim that the Arctic Council is an organization of potentially equal stature to other regional organizations such as the Organization of American States, the Organization for Security and Co-operation in Europe, and the Organization for Asia-Pacific Economic Co-operation. This would be a decidedly premature assessment. The AEPS was widely criticized as an initiative that almost immediately began to wallow in bureaucratic inertia, devoted to monitoring developments and ignoring broader sustainable development issues and, of course, lacking any legal teeth whatsoever. The new council does not advance beyond any of these criticisms, though it may evolve in a conducive manner in the future. Accordingly, it is a great exaggeration at this point to claim that the council is, or even wants to be, the institutional prototype of more cohesive regional integrative mechanisms. In fact, the council provides a quick corrective to compulsive neo-functionalist arguments, though it might evolve to coordinate the activities of an epistemic community in the loose sense. The Arctic Council might eventually move us from what Franklyn Griffiths terms a *co-ordinated political* region towards an *integration* region, characterized by regional community creation and solidarity.[10] But this appears highly unlikely, and it is even less likely that future historians would look upon such a development as the result of Canadian "mission diplomacy."[11]

Indigenous Peoples

In fact, if regional solidarity does become a consistent facet of polar politics, it may be seen most vividly at the non-state level, among the varied inhabitants of the region who have politicized their plight in recent years. The primary (perhaps even *defining*) innovation that characterizes the Arctic Council is the structured inclusion of non-state actors who represent circumpolar indigenous peoples. This status is granted to three groups only: the ICC, the Saami Council (with representation from Scandinavia, Finland, and Russia), and the Association of Indigenous Minorities of the North, Siberia and the Far East of the Russian Federation.

The ICC, with headquarters in Nuuk, was formed in 1977 with Inuit from Alaska, Canada, and Greenland; it was later joined by Russians and has had its NGO status granted by the Economic and Social Council of the United Nations. In 1994 the ICC finally opened an office in Provideniya, Russia, and the Yupik sent delegates to the 1995 meeting at Nome. Few NGOs have been as active as the ICC. In 1988 it received a Global 500 Award from the United Nations Environmental Programme (UNEP) for the development of the Inuit Regional Conservation Strategy, which addressed some 6.4 million square kilometres of area. It has had a strong anti-militarization agenda throughout its political history. In order to sustain the Inuit's right to hunt wildlife (within reasonable limits), the ICC has lobbied many international organizations.

One might even argue that the ICC represents a mechanism of Canadian mission diplomacy, since Canadian governments have supported some of its demands and three of its last four leaders have been Canadian (Mary Simon was followed in 1995 by Rosemarie Kuptana, elected in Nome; she is the president of the Inuit Tapirisat of Canada, which itself represents 35,000 Inuit). Of course, attributing the ICC's relative success to Canadian diplomatic initiative would be stretching things. If anything, the ICC, and the transna-

97

tional links it has effected, should be considered an example of Inuit mission diplomacy! Indeed, one newspaper article even referred to the Arctic Council as an "ICC initiative," though, again, this certainly goes too far.[12] It will be interesting to see the effect of the establishment of a new territory resulting from the Nunavut Land Claim and Accord in 1999, a territory where the Inuit will be a majority.

The larger political question is whether the participation of indigenous groups in the Arctic Council will make a substantial difference. Once acknowledged as key diplomatic players, they will be expected to conform to diplomatic rules that could constrain their effectiveness in challenging policies, military and non-military, that threaten their environmental security. On the other hand, of course, it can be argued that a seat at the table at least gives them a voice.

A Hazy Future?

The diplomatic context of the Arctic Council provides an engrossing tale of community linkage, high-level negotiation, and public profiling. But what problems, on the ground (or, perhaps put another way, under the haze), does the council face? Assuming the most recent rules of procedure and terms of reference for sustainable development (reached finally at Ottawa in early February 1998) survive ministerial approval and eventual public scrutiny, the council will have an opportunity to publicize the problems and attempt to coordinate remedial activity.

Mary Simon recently outlined what she feels are the council's top priorities. She emphasized the grave nature of the environmental threats to circumpolar regions, claiming that, but for the seriousness "of the many threats facing the Arctic, it is unlikely that the Council would have been formed at all."[13] However, other issues are as burning. Simon and many others have stressed the negative impact of a European Union boycott on fur products, for example. One of the most pervasive issues affecting northern peoples relates to animal rights and the subsistence economy, since they have in many areas become dependent on the fur trade. Animal-rights activists will not necessarily like it, but the council will undoubtedly adopt an approach to the issue that accepts trapping and sealing as legitimate ways of life and that promotes the lifting of fur boycotts. A similar stance can be expected on the even more controversial whaling issue.

Another issue relates to the massive changes in Russia, where subsidies to northern communities have been drastically reduced. The northern lifestyle has become a highly expensive one in the age of snowmobiles and imported food. However, as in the Canadian and Alaskan north, indigenous peoples find themselves on land with great potential industrial value; for example, reports of great diamond wealth emerge from Yakutia (Sakha). So the old dilemma resurfaces, but with greater force owing to the new Russia's tendency towards privatization: should native communities have a significant say over the development of local resources and, if so, should they opt for whatever wealth they can acquire through the process or promote a more balanced, conservationist approach? One thing is sure: the ideal of a fully preserved north has no real future, despite the wishes of some urban environmentalists.

We can say with certainty that the southern encroachment on the Arctic will continue. Air traffic has increased over the last few decades and will probably continue to do so since the North Pole route offers certain advantages in east-west transport. Natural gas and oil exploration will rise and fall according to circumstances largely determined elsewhere—the price of oil, perceived costs of reliance on Middle Eastern exports, and the speed with which the transition to a natural gas-based global economy is, or is not, made. Both offshore drilling and Arctic shipping present serious threats to environmental security. Mining activities have been curtailed but may revive, again, according to international markets, unlike in the Antarctic context, where a fifty-year freeze on industrial development is in place within the ATS regime. It is unclear how the Arctic Council can contribute to the prevention of potential environmental damage resulting from all this activity, though it does offer a forum to publicize it. More troubling is that toxic contaminants originate from outside the Arctic (and the same goes for the threats posed by climate change). Though any effort to publicize the Arctic consequences of these much larger-scale questions is welcome, it would be chimerical indeed to expect the Arctic Council to be a decisive factor in charting a course towards a more environmentally benign world economy.

Inherent also in any centralized approach is the issue of diversity. It is perhaps counter-productive to engage in too much generalization, and multilateralism may in fact encourage just this. There are marked differences between the regions in the Arctic, and this will effect any sound plan for environmental management. For example, plans for offshore drilling would have to accommodate differences in the average open-water season, depth of ice, distinctions between first-year and multi-year ice flows, the potential role of artificial islands, and regional wildlife habits, not to mention the concerns of nearby shoreline inhabitants. Differences between the prime off-shore-drilling locations for Canada—the Beaufort Sea, the Sverdrup Basin in the Arctic Islands, and the eastern Arctic (including the Labrador Sea)—are quite pronounced.[14] Shipping lanes will have different impacts on marine life; indigenous communities vary greatly in the extent to which they depend on trading in fur or on whaling as an ancient custom; and the Arctic states have markedly different questions relating to national sovereignty, as Canada's experience indicates. In short, there are so many extraneous variables, some subject to diplomatic negotiation and some not, that the Arctic Council may well end up a frustrated, if celebrated, actor in world affairs. Whether the much vaunted *precautionary principle* has potential as a guiding direction for the council remains to be seen. Whether or not we can apply the same principle to self-declaratory success stories by the federal government remains to be seen also.

Back to the fashionable concept of niche diplomacy: the argument advanced by Potter and others is that, by exercising fiscal prudence, involving NGOs (though which NGOs may be a point of some contention), and maximizing Canada's "inherent advantages," Ottawa can "maintain a high profile on the international stage."[15] It is unclear whether the Arctic Council, which does all these things to some extent, can provide the latter without a commensurate increase in public interest and governmental commitment of resources to Arctic conservation.

NOTES

Thanks to the Social Sciences and Humanities Research Council of Canada for funding; and to several people who have spoken with me

100

on circumpolar affairs, including members of the Canadian Arctic Resources Committee, the Arctic Council Secretariat, the US State Department, many individual researchers who answered an e-mail survey, Bill Graham, and Andrew Cooper. Special thanks go to Melissa Gabler for last-minute research assistance.

1   For the extent of these severe problems, see the Arctic Monitoring and Assessment Programme's six-year "State of the Environment" report on Arctic Pollution issues, released June 1997, <http://www.grida.no/prog/polar/amap/soaer.htm>.

2   O. Young, "Arctic Governance: Bringing the High Latitudes in from the Cold," *International Environmental Affairs* 9/1 (1997), 54-68, 55.

3   A. Cooper, "In Search of Niches: Saying 'Yes' and Saying 'No' in Canada's International Relations," *Canadian Foreign Policy* 3/3 (1995) 1-13; E. Potter, "Niche Diplomacy as Canadian Foreign Policy," *International Journal* 52 (1997), 25-38.

4   Article 234. This provision does not apply to military vessels. See Donat Pharand, *Canada's Arctic Waters in International Law* (Cambridge: Cambridge University Press, 1988), 237.

5   For a concise description of these strategy components and the Canadian role in them, see Rob Huebert, "New Directions in Circumpolar Cooperation: Canada, the Arctic Environmental Protection Strategy, and the Arctic Council," *Canadian Foreign Policy*, 5/2 (1998), 37-57.

6   J. Kirton, "Beyond Bilateralism: U.S.-Canada Co-operation in the Arctic," in W. Westermeyer and K. Shusterich, eds., *U.S. Arctic Interests: The 1980s and 1990s* (New York: Springer Velag, 1984), 308.

7   See J. Merritt, "Factors Influencing Canadian Interest in Greater Non-military Co-operation in the Arctic," in K. Mottola, ed., *The Arctic Challenge: Nordic and Canadian Approaches to Security and Cooperation in an Emerging International Region* (Boulder Colo.:Westview Press, 1988), 281-302, 298.

8   E. Rajakoski, "Multilateral Cooperation to Protect the Arctic Environment: The Finnish Initiative," in Thomas R. Berger, *The Arctic: Choices for Peace and Security* (West Vancouver: Gordon Soules Book Publishers, 1989), 52-9.

9 Department of Foreign Affairs and International Trade (DFAIT) Press Release, Government of Canada, 19 September 1996.

10 See F. Griffiths, "Challenge and Leadership in the Arctic," in E. Dosman, ed., *Sovereignty and Security in the Arctic* (London: Routledge, 1989), 211-27.

11 Without doubt, *Canadians* have played key roles here. Two names in particular stand out: Mary Simon and Walter Slipchenko, the executive director of the council secretariat, who has laboured for years in Ottawa to establish circumpolar links and who was kind enough to discuss his work and the council with me (albeit in diplomatically guarded terms!).

12 J. George, "Canadian Inuit reach out to Siberia's northern people," *Globe and Mail*, 17 August 1995, A11.

13 M. Simon, "Circumpolar Nations Tackle Big Jobs with Arctic Council," speech to the Canada Club of Toronto, 4 November 1996; published in *Canadian Speeches: Issues of the Day* 10/9 (1997), 26-30, 27.

14 See E. Dosman, "Arctic Seas: Environmental Policy and Natural Resource Development," in O.P. Dwivedi, ed., *Resources and the Environment: Policy Perspectives for Canada* (Toronto: McClelland & Stewart, 1980), 198-215.

15 E. Potter, "Niche Diplomacy as Canadian Foreign Policy," 37.

Politico-Diplomatic Initiatives: Some Criteria For Success

Louis A. Delvoie

The reasons that prompt governments to take politico-diplomatic initiatives are varied indeed. Among the major variables are foreign-policy priorities, international events and developments, and, not least, the personalities and interests of individual political leaders. The issues addressed, the objectives pursued, and the degree of success achieved are also highly varied, as the chapters in this book make clear. But are there any hard and fast generic rules to guide a government in deciding whether or not to launch an initiative or in assessing its prospects for success? I think that the answer is no, precisely because of the number of variables in play. I do, however, believe that it is possible to identify some essentially technical conditions or criteria which may be of use to governments in their decision making. Meeting these criteria will not necessarily ensure success, but failure to meet a number of them may well produce the opposite result.

In this very preliminary offering of ten possible criteria which I believe merit consideration, I have drawn most of my illustrations from the Trudeau era, and especially from the Trudeau "peace initiative" of 1983-4.[1] This is done deliberately in order to avoid repetition of material already available in the more contemporary case studies included in this volume.

First, *the initiative must enjoy the wholehearted support of the Canadian government.* It is usually difficult enough to persuade foreign governments of the merits of a particular initiative, but doubly so if it becomes known (as it inevitably does) that the Canadian government itself is divided on the question. This became evident during the Trudeau peace initiative, which was viewed with deep scepticism, if not downright hostility, by many senior ministers and senior officials, who saw it as a quixotic venture likely to have a detrimental effect on Canada's relations with the United States and other NATO allies. The same had been true of Trudeau's earlier pursuit of a "contractual link" with the European Community, which did not enjoy the support of the principal economic ministers and departments in Ottawa.[2]

Second, *the initiative must be based on a clear-headed assessment of the pros and cons.* In the case of the Trudeau peace initiative, no such assessment had been undertaken in any depth. The reality and the repercussions of the hostile reactions of the governments of the United States, Britain, and India to different aspects of the initiative had not been properly evaluated in advance and had to be dealt with on an ad hoc and defensive basis, to the detriment of the initiative's momentum and effectiveness.

Third, *the initiative must be based on a clear-headed assessment of Canada's relative influence.* A case in point is the decision of the Canadian government, announced in January 1998, to send a special envoy to investigate the deadly and bloody civil war taking place in Algeria.[3] While Canada has worked fairly assiduously at developing its bilateral relationship with Algeria, and while Algeria ranks as Canada's largest export market in Africa and the Middle East, there is little reason to believe that Canada by itself occupies a position of sufficient influence in Algeria to do anything meaningful to attenuate the effects of the conflict. On the one hand, countries such as France, Germany, Italy, and Spain are of far greater importance to Algeria, both economically and politically, than is Canada. And yet the European Union has been able to make no headway whatsoever on the Algerian problem. On the other hand, Algeria is a country that has always jealously guarded its national sovereignty and categorically rejected all forms of interference in its internal affairs.

Fourth, *the government must have available to it a reservoir of relevant diplomatic and technical expertise.* This point is perhaps too self-evident or too trite to require much elaboration, but it does impose some limitations. Canada may be well placed to take initiatives dealing with Arctic waters or transatlantic relations, but it would be severely handicapped if it sought to promote projects for the protection of tropical rainforests or the eradication of yellow fever. In terms of expertise, Canada's comparative advantage will generally lie where its national and international experience and interests lie.

Fifth, *an initiative must be thoroughly prepared and planned.* Prime Minister Trudeau gave his officials less than two weeks to do the substantive preparation of his peace initiative, and the decision making and implementation were to be squeezed into a period of less than three months. (In the end, this stretched to nearly five months because of unforeseen circumstances.) The result was an initiative launched with insufficient attention to detail and with no opportunity to lay the diplomatic groundwork which might have assured it a warmer welcome in allied capitals. No governments, and this is especially true of those of the major powers, like to be surprised or blind-sided by the unilateral actions of others. And yet the governments of NATO countries were given only two or three days' advance warning of the public launch of the Trudeau initiative, and those of the Soviet Union and China none at all.

Sixth, *the purposes of the initiative must be clear, simple, and readily understandable to governments, publics, and the media alike.* The central purpose of the Trudeau initiative, the restoration of political dialogue between East and West and especially the superpowers, met this criterion admirably. Unfortunately, the total content of the initiative did not. Trudeau chose to pursue simultaneously a series of essentially disconnected arms-control proposals, some of which were highly technical in nature, for example, limitations on the mobility of new strategic missiles or bans on the deployment of high-altitude anti-satellite systems. In sharp contrast to this was the Canadian government's recent campaign to ban anti-personnel land mines; its purpose could be understood by the meanest intelligence, and its humanitarian goal was almost guaranteed to garner widespread support.

Seventh, *the Canadian government should enjoy a pool of relevant diplomatic credit in some key capitals.* In the case of the Trudeau peace initiative, this was clearly a commodity in short supply. A consistent critic of NATO, as the prime minister who had or-

105

dained a sharp cutback in Canada's contribution to the Alliance, and as a leader who had displayed only a sporadic interest in East-West security affairs, Trudeau enjoyed little credibility in most Western capitals when it came time to rally support for his initiative. The fact that he was by this time the longest-serving head of government in NATO was insufficient to make up for these shortfalls, let alone overcome the resistance so evident in Washington and London.

Eighth, *the identification of potential allies and the process of coalition-building must take place at an early stage in the initiative.* There are few, if any, areas of interest in which Canada can hope to mount and conduct a successful initiative unilaterally. The rapid constitution of a coalition of the so-called "like-minded" is usually essential, not least in order to create both the reality and the image of support and momentum. This in turn will lead other less interested or less sympathetic parties at least to take note and consider whether or not they should jump on the bandwagon. This was admirably achieved in the anti-personnel land mines campaign, far less so in Trudeau's peace initiative or in his efforts to foster global negotiations as part of a putative north-south dialogue.

Ninth, *the initiative should be characterized by firmness as to purpose and flexibility as to means.* The purpose of the initiative should be spelled out in clear terms if it is to have any chance of garnering public and government support, but it should not be stated in such detail that it makes tactical changes of course seem like reversals or retreats. The dynamics and duration of an initiative, as well as the totally unforeseen, may dictate departures from the plan of action as originally formulated, and the plan should make allowances for this, for example, allowing the result of the initiative to be enshrined in an International Committee of the Red Cross protocol rather than a UN convention.

Tenth, *the sponsor of an initiative should know when to quit.* Flogging dead horses is as counterproductive in international relations as it is in interpersonal relations. Recognizing in a timely way that an initiative has run its course and is not going to be further advanced by additional activity is essential to retaining the credibility required to mount other initiatives in other areas at other times. Thus, in the 1970s, the Canadian government became thoroughly disenchanted with the performance of the head of a major UN agency and sought to have him replaced with a Canadian candidate. The campaign mounted by the Canadian government was broad and vigorous but in the end unsuccessful. The incumbent was re-elected, but the Canadian government kept up its campaign against him for several years, to the point that even sympathetic officials in foreign countries became at first amused, then bored, and finally annoyed by the never-ending Canadian diplomatic démarches on the subject.[4] At the very least, this episode did little to enhance the reputation of Canadian diplomacy.

As I come to the end of this short decalogue, I am reminded of an anecdote told about Napoleon. The story has it that a group of his courtiers were trying to persuade the emperor to entrust a certain command to a certain general. They spoke at great length about the general's qualities as a strategist and tactician, about his mastery of logistics, and about his leadership abilities. After listening to all they had to say, Napoleon simply asked "Yes, but is he lucky?" Well, luck can be as important to the success of politico-diplomatic campaigns as it is to military campaigns. Prime Minister Trudeau was the victim of bad luck in his peace initiative. In his efforts to restore political dialogue between Moscow and Washington, he was hobbled by the fact that he could not secure an invitation to visit Moscow because the ageing Soviet leader of the day was ailing and dying. On the other hand, the Canadian government's campaign to ban land mines enjoyed an extraordinary stroke of good luck when the cause was espoused in visible ways by one of the world's pre-eminent media stars, Princess Diana. And her subsequent tragic death in a car accident, which became the media event of the decade, did much to boost the fortunes of all of the causes in which she had taken an interest. While luck cannot readily be factored in to initial decisions about whether or not to undertake a politico-diplomatic initiative, it can certainly have a real impact on the outcome.

NOTES

1   The Trudeau peace initiative is described and analysed in the following: J.L Granatstein and R. Bothwell, *Pirouette: Pierre Trudeau and Canadian Foreign Policy* (Toronto: University of

Toronto Press, 1990), 363-76; John Kirton, "Trudeau and the Diplomacy of Peace," *International Perspectives* (July/August, 1984); H. von Riekhoff and J. Sigler, "The Trudeau Peace Initiative: The Politics of Reversing the Arms Race," in B. Tomlin and M. Molot, eds., *Canada among Nations 1984: A Time of Transition* (Toronto: James Lorimer and Company, 1985). For Trudeau's own assessment of the initiative, see Ivan Head and Pierre Trudeau, *The Canadian Way* (Toronto: McClelland & Stewart, 1995), 292-309.

[2]   On this subject, see Granatstein and Bothwell, *Pirouette,* 158-72. See also Charles Pentland, "Europe 1992 and the Canadian Response," in F.O. Hampson and C.J. Maule, eds., *Canada among Nations 1990-91: After the Cold War* (Ottawa: Carleton University Press, 1991), 127-9.

[3]   See Department of Foreign Affairs and International Trade (DFAIT), *News Release* no. 1/98 and no. 9/98 (Ottawa, 1998).

[4]   This recounting of the episode is based on the author's recollection of events which occurred while he was a member of the Canadian foreign service, working both in Ottawa and abroad. He is not aware of any published accounts of this particular campaign.

Contributors

David Black
Department of Political Science
Dalhousie University

Andrew F. Cooper
Department of Political Science
University of Waterloo

Louis A. Delvoie
Centre For International Relations
Queen's University

John R. English
Department of History
University of Waterloo

Geoffrey Hayes
Department of History
University of Waterloo

Miguel de Larrinaga
Department of Political Science
University of Ottawa

Kim Richard Nossal
Department of Political Science
McMaster University

Evan H. Potter
Canadian Foreign Policy
The Norman Paterson School of International Affairs
Carleton University

Claire Turenne Sjolander
Department of Political Science
University of Ottawa

Heather A. Smith
International Studies Program
University of Northern British Columbia

Peter J. Stoett
Department of Political Science
Concordia University

110

Index

AGMV
MARQUIS

Québec, Canada
2000